WOMAN

New Century Theology

Other books in this series include:

WOMAN

Tina Beattie

New Century Theology

continuum
LONDON • NEW YORK

CONTINUUM
The Tower Building, 11 York Road, London SE1 7NX
15 East 26th Street, New York, NY 10010

www.continuumbooks.com

First published 2003

British Library Cataloguing-in-Publication Data
A catalogue record for this book is available from the British Library.

ISBN 0 – 8264–5703 –7

Typeset by Continuum
Printed and bound in Great Britain by Cromwell Press, Wiltshire

Contents

For Jade and Asia

Do I imagine reality
Or does the real imagine me?
Unimaginable imaginer
What part does the imagined play?

Kathleen Raine [1]

[1] Kathleen Raine, 'Do I Imagine Reality?'
in *The Collected Poems of Kathleen Raine*
(Washington DC: Counterpoint, 2001), p. 325.

Preface

In writing a book like this, it is always a dilemma as to how much personal reflection one should include. On the one hand, theology is an academic discipline that demands a level of objectivity and rational enquiry, and it therefore requires a different approach from devotional writing. But on the other hand, theology is a profoundly subjective discipline. It is, in the phrase of St Anselm, 'faith seeking understanding', and therefore it constitutes a struggle for meaning played out in the space between an individual believer's life and an intellectual tradition with an established history of methods and meanings. For women theologians, this task has an added complication in so far as the theological tradition has been almost exclusively developed by men, and therefore its universal claims about human nature and God mask the fact that it is in fact a one-sided, androcentric tradition that has failed to explore the relationship between the human and the divine from the perspective of women.

As a professional theologian, I am aware of a duty both to the Church and to the academic community to work with a sense of discipline, rigour and faithfulness to scholarly criteria. But as a woman caught up in the struggle for symbolic transformation and new ways of being in the world in this age of astonishing opportunity and crisis, my own unresolved questions and dilemmas remain part of the text.

There are therefore many loose ends, many unresolved
issues, and perhaps areas of manifest confusion and ambiguity in what follows. I hope these reflect genuine areas of
bewilderment in my own understanding, rather than simply the convolutions of a prosaic theological style. As far as
possible, I have tried to write with clarity and transparency
for a non-academic readership, but I have also found myself
grappling with profound theological questions that are tangled and difficult to unravel. When this happens I ask the
reader to join me in the labour to give birth to new meanings that we cannot yet clearly see or recognize.

My approach is deeply influenced by Catholic theology
and symbolism, because as a convert from Protestantism I
remain intrigued and compelled by the complex world of
Roman Catholicism. As one who lacks faith in the abstract,
I cannot give intellectual assent to a set of rational propositions about God, and I have no firm conviction that the
Christian story must be true. But the Catholic tradition's
way of speaking about and worshipping God resonates
through history and forward into eternity, weaving into
the textures and meanings of western culture a narrative
that is materially expressed in the languages we speak and
the spaces we inhabit. This tradition gives shape to the
ultimate questions about life, even as God remains that
elusive, inescapable absence around which all possible
meanings are shaped. In experiencing this absence in my
own life, I sometimes recognize what Jacques Lacan calls
jouissance. This is a psychological state that arises out of a
haunting void, and that occasionally erupts into an erotic
ecstasy of being which feels like a dissolution into the
infinite. Nothing matters and everything matters, because
life becomes for a moment a boundless Yes. Lacan associates *jouissance* with female mysticism, but perhaps the
closest modern literary equivalent is the ending of James
Joyce's *Ulysses*, with Molly Bloom's orgasmic cascade of words.

Growing up as a Presbyterian in Zambia, my childhood experiences of Christianity offered no opening into such sensual exuberance of faith, but I knew that somewhere out there, beyond the pared down austerity of our little kirk in which we Scottish colonials acted out our nostalgic rites, there was something else which wasn't properly Christian, but which was full of mystery and colour and the constant possibility of the miraculous. It was called Catholicism. By the time I was ready for secondary school, the Dominican Convent was one of the few good girls' schools left in Zambia, so, after much discussion and soul-searching, my parents decided to send me there.

It is important not to underestimate what a powerful impression being educated by a community of religious women motivated by a vision beyond marriage and family life can make on an adolescent girl. Today the press is full of stories of abusive priests and nuns, of childhoods destroyed by the brutality of Catholic schools and institutions. My own experience was different. Certainly, a few of the sisters were deeply dotty, and some of them were forbiddingly stern. But my abiding memory of those years is of women who inspired me with their strength, their wisdom and their commitment to the girls in their care. It was there that I learned values that, after the rebellion of my teenage years, I have found myself reclaiming and wanting to live by as I have matured.

With hindsight, I recognize that those were heady days in the Catholic Church. I had never heard of the Second Vatican Council, but I attended that school from 1966 to 1970, as the revolution that had happened in Rome was slowly dawning on the Catholic world. What I was experiencing was the exhilaration of a community of women who were discovering possibilities in their faith that had never been open to them before. There was an infectious enthusiasm to those years, and it left a deep impression on me.

So, while seeking to sustain an intellectual engagement with an established theological tradition, the following cannot and does not claim to be a definitive theology of woman, nor to be a story of Everywoman. It is one theologian's personal struggle to understand what it might mean to be a woman, if one asks that question in an existential and intellectual commitment to the Christian story of salvation understood in the language, symbols and sacraments of Roman Catholicism, but also informed by the possibilities and challenges of the modern world. As we move into a postmodern age with so many shifting, transient opportunities and so many different visions and voices, I believe that women need to draw on all the resources of the past to create the possibility of a future not of violent change brought about by denial and repression, but of the ongoing transformation of human life through all the ages and stages of history. For Christians, this means weaving together a plurality of conversations and dialogues involving many different traditions, cultures and beliefs, while constantly seeking to deepen and enrich the Christian story as it is played out between a mythical beginning and a promised ending, in a community that discovers its meaning, its purpose and its material reality in the story of Christ and the Church.

Introduction

I once went into a university bookshop looking for Tom Paine's *The Rights of Man* and Mary Wollstonecraft's *A Vindication of the Rights of Woman*. I found Paine in the philosophy section, but I could find nothing by Wollstonecraft. When I asked the assistant, he checked his computer and said, 'Wollstonecraft is in the fiction section.'

Some might argue that Wollstonecraft's philosophical vision of women's rights is not a fiction but a goal that is being realized in the modern world, even if progress is slow. But Wollstonecraft belongs to the dawn of an age that is now in its twilight years. She was present at the birth of modernity, that great transformation in European consciousness known as the Enlightenment. This was when the traditional authorities of Church and monarchy were yielding to new democratic values in which authority was vested not in a divinely sanctioned social hierarchy but in universal reason. Wollstonecraft shared with the philosophers of the Enlightenment a belief that through the power of reason and the cultivation of virtue, it would be possible to build a new social order based on collective values of freedom, justice and equality. In particular, she explored these ideas in critical engagement with the work of Jean-Jacques Rousseau. She pointed to a fundamental flaw in Rousseau's reasoning because he sought to retain a hierarchical division between the sexes, based on a highly romanticized (and, argues Wollstonecraft, lascivious), view of femininity. Men would be the educated citizens and rulers of the new society, while women would be consigned to their traditional roles of submissive wives and mothers, whose education need extend only so far as teaching them the ploys of seduction and obedience that they would need to keep their husbands contented and sexually sated. Wollstonecraft saw that any philosophy that sought to liberate men from the tyranny of unelected power must extend to liberating women from the tyranny of men. It was her passionate advocacy of this belief that made her the pioneer of modern feminism, and that led to her being labelled by the men of her time as 'a hyena in petticoats' and 'a philosophizing serpent'.

But it is interesting to speculate as to what Wollstonecraft might have said about feminism and women's rights at the beginning of the twenty-first century. For all our rhetoric about equality, rights and choice, are we any closer to achieving her vision, or have we perhaps gone down an altogether different route, so that her appeals to divine justice and universal reason might be seen as anachronistic or irrelevant to women today? As the Enlightenment vision of modernity fragments into a myriad postmodern fictions, fantasies and relativities, and as the Christian tradition fades into a distant cultural memory, what, if anything, constitutes truth in contemporary society? And if we have no shared concept of truth, how can we discuss questions of equality, rights and justice? Is it still possible to understand ourselves in relation to universal moral laws, or do we come to know ourselves only by delving ever more deeply into our private, inner worlds, seeking security in an authentic self beyond the restless transience of the societies around us? Can we make sense of the cultural and ethical labyrinths that we inhabit, or should we give up and surrender ourselves to the parody and the pathos of lives from which the ultimate questions have been banished – Who am I? Why do I exist? How should I live?

This book seeks to reintroduce those questions by asking how they apply to women in the context of the Christian tradition. It offers an exploration of the ways in which Christianity has influenced western ideas about womanhood to such an extent that, even although feminism is largely (although by no means exclusively) a post-Christian movement, it owes many of its insights to Christianity. However, secularism often cultivates a suspicious if not hostile attitude to religion, and in the case of secular feminism this takes the form of a sustained resistance to any form of Christian social or historical analysis or theological reflection. While feminist theologians have a wide-ranging engagement with secular feminist theory, few secular feminists even acknowledge the existence of religious feminism. In addition, some feminist theology has been highly critical of the Christian tradition while adopting an over-simplified approach to its historical and cultural diversity, so that feminist theologians sometimes fail to acknowledge the extent to which Christianity has had a liberating as well as an oppressive influence on women's lives. I hope that this book will be a resource for those who seek a more holistic and integrated approach to the question of woman, by listening to the voices of the many women through the ages who have questioned, challenged or affirmed these beliefs in their own quest for identity and meaning, including Wollstonecraft.

With this in mind, the chapters are written as interconnecting narratives. Each takes a particular situation or question involving women – some historical, some contemporary – and uses that as the basis for a theological reflection on women's lives from the perspective of the Christian tradition. Such ideas of narrative and story-telling belong more comfortably in a premodern or post-

modern worldview than in that of rationalizing modernity.
If we are to live meaningful lives, then we need to rediscover the language of poetry, storytelling and myth-mak-
ing, not as a way of escaping from reality into fiction, but
as a way of suffusing reality with meaning, hope and
vision. This entails cultivating forms of understanding in
which past, present and future are creatively woven into a
coherent story about who we are in the world, both in
terms of our individual lives and in terms of our shared
histories and traditions. For those whose social identities
have been shaped by western culture, this means recognizing the extent to which Christian beliefs, images and symbols continue to influence our cultural and ethical values,
not least with regard to our sexual identities and relationships. But it also means respecting the syncretistic relationship between Christianity and modern liberalism,
which, however great its flaws and failings, has offered
women an alternative set of values from which to question
and challenge some of the more repressive aspects of religious traditions, including Christianity.

Conservative Christians sometimes point to feminism
as the source of all the social ills of modern society.
Feminists are destroying the family, preaching heresy,
encouraging sexual immorality, and tearing apart the fabric of society. There is a humorous postcard that carries a
quotation from the American Christian televangelist, Pat
Robertson: 'Feminism encourages women to leave their
husbands, kill their children, practice witchcraft, destroy
capitalism and become lesbians.' But Christian feminism is
part of a continuous tradition in the Church. While contemporary feminism offers new insights and perspectives,
many of its values and ideas are not fundamentally new.
What is new is that these are no longer isolated visions
emanating from deep within a male-dominated tradition
that has the power to silence women's voices and banish

their memories from history. From this point of view, the encounter between feminism and the Christian faith does not represent two separate or conflicting stories so much as two hopeful themes within a more multifaceted and open-ended story about the world.

As our social and intellectual horizons broaden, we have every reason to be sceptical about any theory or belief that claims to offer an ultimate or comprehensive explanation of life. We know that the human story is infinitely more varied and complex – and perhaps also more tragic – than our ancestors acknowledged. We live in an era that is terrifying in its capacity for destruction, but which is also exhilarating in its potential to expand and enrich our ways of understanding one another and the world around us. It is an age of flickering promise and dark intimations of despair, mediated to us by way of an ever-expanding global communications network that binds us together more intimately than ever before, even as we face forces that divide us more violently than ever before. In all this hope and confusion, we are surrounded by religious and secular arguments and debates, promises and threats, which can make the quest for meaning too confusing to bother with. Yet I believe that our humanity is inseparable from our creativity, and our creativity is oriented towards the expression of our longing for meaning, beauty and truth, and for that transcendent mystery that some refer to as God. That these are elusive desires, hard to articulate, impossible to capture except in transient moments of grace, makes it more, rather than less important that we should listen to the multitude of voices from other times and places, who have shared our quest and left us with their unfinished stories and their unanswered questions.

While women have featured widely in writings about the human condition and the meaning of life, until the twentieth century these were, with relatively few exceptions, the writings of men thinking about women, rather than women thinking about themselves. Even when women did write about themselves, they often did so with a consciousness shaped by an androcentric worldview, in which they accepted more or less uncritically the positions assigned to them and the characteristics attributed to them by men. But scholars today are excavating the historical record and making it possible, perhaps for the first time in history, to listen to a collection of women's voices that extends across time and space, and to some extent across religions and traditions, so that for the first time it is feasible to ask what a Christian theology of woman written by women might look like, when it is rooted in tradition but also dynamic and open to future possibilities.

Feminist consciousness refers to a process by which women are recognized not as the objects but as the subjects of history and society. This means looking at the world in such a way that our questions, observations and ways of understanding are shaped by an attentiveness to the presence of women as half of humankind, and an awareness of how much has been lost or denied in the exclusion of that half of humanity from the authorship of the human story. In other words, while women have always been present in history and society, only now are significant numbers of women beginning to participate actively in the creation and interpretation of our religious, cultural and philosophical narratives.

But attentiveness to the diversity of narrative identities and relationships cautions against constructing a monolithic theory or theology of woman. It means rather listening to a multitude of different voices, to find the ways in which the story of Christ and the Church resonates in many ways through the histories and traditions that have patterned the lives of Christian women. Our sense of self is shaped in subtle relationships and influences, so that social, religious and domestic environments are complex worlds of opportunity and challenge wherein we become bearers of infinitely nuanced and intricate meanings and memories. Women have been made and destroyed, inspired and crushed by Christianity over the centuries. The story of woman in the Christian tradition is too complex to lend itself to any kind of value judgement or moral evaluation based on the narrow criteria of contemporary feminism. The growing literature that seeks to retrieve and reinterpret the stories of women from the perspectives of history, fiction and biography attests to this fecundity that resists any reduction to a straightforward moral message.

Dana Sobel's exquisite book, *Galileo's Daughter*, is actually the story of two daughters, not one. The girls, Virginia and Livia, were born out of wedlock to Galileo's mistress, Marina Gamba, and their father put them into a convent for their own protection in 1613 when they were thirteen and twelve respectively, because the circumstances of their birth made it unlikely that they would find husbands. Virginia took the name Suor Maria Celeste when she entered religious life, inspired by her father's celestial interests, while Livia took the name Suor Arcangela. Maria Celeste's correspondence with her father suggests a woman of extraordinary intelligence, faith and determination, who from behind the walls of the convent was able to exert widespread influence over her community and her father's affairs. Sobel writes, 'No detectable strife ever disturbed the affectionate relationship between Galileo and his daughter. Theirs is not a tale of abuse or rejection or intentional stifling of abilities. Rather, it is a love story, a tragedy and a mystery.'[1] Maria Celeste was a devoted and faithful supporter of her father throughout his struggles with the Church authorities, and her death from dysentery in 1634 plunged Galileo into desolation. But Arcangela seems to have had a more depressive personality and was less well

suited to convent life. Although she outlived her sister, she
suffered frequent ill health and bouts of depression. The
story of these two sisters, situated at a pivotal point in the
history of western Europe, is a reminder that a situation
that might provide one woman with an environment in
which to flourish and grow, can for another represent an
imprisonment of the spirit. In a similar fashion, Michèle
Roberts' novel, *Daughters of the House*, is inspired by the
relationship between St Thérèse of Lisieux and her sister,
Leonie.[2] The fictional sisters in the novel represent two radically different experiences of faith, again suggesting the
ways in which women's reactions to their spiritual environments and religious upbringings are the product of
immensely complex personality differences, family relationships and sibling rivalries.

If, then, we acknowledge that such profound religious
differences occur even between sisters with similar childhood experiences, it becomes clear that the word 'woman'
evokes countless existential possibilities in its religious
contexts. In approaching the question of woman in the
Christian tradition, one must explore a story that has been
played out in a space of encounter between the largely consistent and frequently denigratory theology of womanhood
that has been perpetuated by Catholic and Protestant theologians alike, and the infinitely varied ways in which
Christian women have lived and expressed themselves in
intricate relationships of conformity to and rebellion
against the dominant theological tradition. So my appeal is
not to women's experience *per se*, but to the ways in which
women no less than men have grappled with the symbols,
values and stories of the Christian faith in order to give
coherence and meaning to their experiences of life.

Although my ideas are influenced by feminism, I also try
to set aside the agenda of contemporary feminism in order
to ask, in the context of the Christian tradition, 'What does

a woman want?' When Freud asked that question he did so in bafflement and perplexity, acknowledging that his forty years of psychoanalysing women had not given him an answer. Luce Irigaray, feminist and *femme fatale* of Freudian psychoanalysis, suggests that Freud failed to find an answer because he did not know how to listen. In what follows I try to listen and learn, and I ask what insights Christianity has to offer for women who have in every era sought to discover a sense of dignity, joy and hope in the eyes of God and in the eyes of their fellow human beings, while struggling against a pervasive cultural and religious milieu that has consistently devalued and trivialized women.

I begin with Wollstonecraft because she epitomizes many of the unresolved dilemmas and conflicting values that still present themselves when one asks what it means to be a woman in the modern world. These questions involve profound philosophical issues about the meaning and purpose of human existence, and they encompass arguments about sexual and social ethics, identity, duties and responsibilities, and ways of relating to and caring for one another and the environment around us. Although philosophers and seers have been exploring the question of man for at least three millennia, Wollstonecraft was an innovator in the modern world of ideas because she was the first to address herself specifically to the question of woman, and it would be nearly two hundred years before her work would find acceptance and recognition by women.

---

[1] Dava Sobel, *Galileo's Daughter* (London: Fourth Estate, 2000), p. 9.
[2] See Michèle Roberts, *Daughters of the House* (London: Virago Press, 1993).

1
Enlightenment Woman and God

The only solid foundation for morality appears to be the character of the Supreme Being; the harmony of which arises from a balance of attributes; – and, to speak with reverence, one attribute seems to imply the *necessity* of another. He must be just, because He is wise; He must be good, because He is omnipotent. For to exalt one attribute at the expense of another equally noble and necessary, bears the stamp of the warped reason of man – the homage of passion. Man, accustomed to bow down to power in his savage state, can seldom divest himself of this barbarous prejudice, even when civilization determines how much superior mental is to bodily strength; and his reason is clouded by these crude opinions, even when he thinks of the Deity. His omnipotence is made to swallow up, or preside over His other attributes, and those mortals are supposed to limit His power irreverently, who think that it must be regulated by His wisdom.

> I disclaim that specious humility which, after investigating nature, stops at the Author. The High and Lofty One, who inhabiteth eternity, doubtless possesses many attributes of which we can form no conception; but Reason tells me that they cannot clash with those I adore – and I am compelled to listen to her voice.
>
> Mary Wollstonecraft, 1759–1797 [1]

woman who lived on the threshold of the modern world, her
ideas belong in the related realms of Christian theology and
Enlightenment philosophy, her rationality is grounded in an
ardent but questioning faith, and her personal relationships
and struggles suggest a woman whose very existence was
torn apart by the conflicting desires, ideals and physical
realities that women must negotiate if they seek personal
and social fulfilment in a time of changing values and
visions. As a revolutionary philosopher, Wollstonecraft's
confidence in the power of reason to bring about a transformation in the sexual and social values of her time was shak-
en but not destroyed by her own experiences of love, motherhood, suffering and loss. Perhaps her eventual acknowledgement that 'we reason deeply, when we forcibly feel'[2]
could be described as the feminization of Enlightenment
philosophy, resonating as it does with some of the insights
and arguments of contemporary feminist thinkers.

Many feminists argue that the western man of reason,
who has his origins in Greek philosophy but who reached
his apotheosis in the European Enlightenment and its
aftermath, is an ideological construct which ascribes to the
masculine subject disembodied attributes of autonomy,
rationality and freedom, while projecting onto his feminine
'other' attributes of relationality, irrationality and dependence, closely identified with female sexuality and embodiment. Feminists argue that sexual justice demands that
both men and women go beyond such stereotypes, to discover less dualistic, more integrated ways of understanding ourselves as sexual beings with a shared capacity to
reason and to feel, to experience both autonomy and
dependence, identity and relationality, embodiment and

transcendence. This means challenging the ways in which traditional gender values still govern our sexual and social relationships in subtle but pervasive ways. For example, Rudyard Kipling's poem, 'If', was elected Britain's favourite poem in 1995 in a poll conducted by BBC television, suggesting that its vision of manhood has a continuing ability to inspire. But does Kipling's man really represent admirable moral qualities for men and women today?

> If you can keep your head when all about you
> Are losing theirs and blaming it on you;
> If you can trust yourself when all men doubt you,
> But make allowance for their doubting too:
> If you can wait and not be tired by waiting,
> Or, being lied about, don't deal in lies,
> Or, being hated, don't give way to hating,
> And yet don't look too good, nor talk too wise;
>
> If you can dream – and not make dreams your master;
> If you can think – and not make thoughts your aim;
> If you can meet with Triumph and Disaster
> And treat those two imposters just the same;
> If you can bear to hear the truth you've spoken
> Twisted by knaves to make a trap for fools,
> Or watch the things you gave your life to broken,
> And stoop and build 'em up with worn-out tools;
>
> If you can make one heap of all your winnings
> And risk it on one turn of pitch-and-toss,
> And lose, and start again at your beginnings
> And never breathe a word about your loss;
> If you can force your heart and nerve and sinew
> To serve your turn long after they are gone,
> And so hold on when there is nothing in you
> Except the Will which says to them: 'Hold on!'

If you can talk with crowds and keep your virtue,
Or walk with kings – nor lose the common touch;
If neither foes nor loving friends can hurt you;
If all men count with you, but none too much;
If you can fill the unforgiving minute
With sixty seconds' worth of distance run –
Yours is the Earth and everything that's in it,
And – which is more – you'll be a Man, my son!

In leading Britain into America's war with Iraq in 2003, Prime Minister Tony Blair exhibited Kipling's qualities of self-assured and stoic manhood in the face of almost universal international opposition. For many of us, this was a sinister scenario in which unflinching moral conviction translated into hubristic and unaccountable power. The moral qualities celebrated by Kipling are not unambiguously good, and indeed one could say that they mask considerable weaknesses of character. While a level of emotional equilibrium is undoubtedly desirable if one is to function as a sane and moral being in the world, there is something chilling about the idea of an individual who seeks to go through life so detached from others that he can disengage himself from all sense of susceptibility to those around him. The quest for imperial power and domination is perhaps the darker side of Kipling's man, who achieves ownership of the earth and everything in it through an ambitious individualism that seeks to transcend any sense of need, vulnerability, or dependence. Such men are in fact profoundly *dependent*, for they rely on others – wives, mothers, children, servants – to attend to their emotional and physical needs. To deny such dependence and the cost it exacts is a form of moral failure, for the illusion of perfect self-sufficiency depends on a high degree of emotional insensitivity and social and sexual exploitation.

Many feminist thinkers, from Wollstonecraft to Simone de Beauvoir, have suggested that equality with men will bring about greater freedom and justice for women. Wollstonecraft argued that women as well as men needed to be educated in self-discipline, reason and virtuous living, if relationships between the sexes were to be based on mutual respect and friendship, rather than on male domination and female degradation. For de Beauvoir, women had to be liberated from the psychological and physical limitations of their sex, including motherhood, if they were to enjoy the same existential freedoms and fulfilments described by her lover and philosophical soul-mate, Jean Paul Sartre. Yet the lives of both women beg complex questions about the extent to which men's philosophical ideals suffice to articulate the visions and experiences of women. Both women struggled to reconcile their intellectual beliefs with the realities of their sexual and emotional relationships, and indeed it seems that the priority of these relationships sometimes threatened to overwhelm their carefully argued philosophical principles. Although, like Wollstonecraft, de Beauvoir ranks as one of the great pioneers of feminism, much of her adult life was spent in Sartre's shadow, meeting his intellectual and physical needs and negotiating a space of survival for herself among his many other loves and relationships.

In Wollstonecraft's case, her life story was one of the most profound psychological, emotional and moral involvement with other people's lives. She dedicated her early adult years to the care of her dying mother, and then assumed emotional and financial responsibility for her father and siblings, and for various friends in need. She travelled to Portugal to be with her pregnant friend, Fanny, whose death in childbirth haunted Wollstonecraft with a sense of bereavement for the rest of her life. She was motivated by a sense of moral rigour, social justice and solidarity with the poor that informs all her work. But she was also a passionate and highly strung woman, who could not ultimately divorce her philosophy from her personal feelings and circumstances. Thus Wollstonecraft's writings constitute an intricate and multi-layered narrative, combining philosophy, theology, social commentary, travelogue and autobiography. It is a narrative that tells of a sustained struggle to negotiate the sometimes painful distance between what she believed to be possible in terms of reason, morality and justice, and what she knew to be the disordered realities of relationships in her private life as well as in the societies she lived in and observed.

Wollstonecraft, born in 1759, was one of six children. Her father was an impoverished farmer, and her long-suffering mother bore the brunt of her husband's frustration in an abusive and violent marriage. She had an itinerant childhood, gleaning what education she could as her family moved from one failed farm to another. As a young woman she worked in a variety of jobs as a governess and lady's companion, as well as establishing a school in Newington Green in 1783. This brought her into contact with liberal thinkers and nonconformist ministers who would have a lasting influence on her intellectual development, and whose ideas contributed to her emergent feminism. Wollstonecraft settled in London in 1788, where she became part of a radical group that included Thomas Paine, William Blake and the philosopher William Godwin. She wrote several works of fiction and social commentary, and her most famous book, *A Vindication of the Rights of Woman*, was published in 1792.

Like many of her intellectual contemporaries, Wollstonecraft travelled to France to experience the Revolution and she stayed in Paris throughout the Terror. It was there that she fell in love with an American businessman and property speculator, Gilbert Imlay, and in May 1794 she gave birth to a daughter, Fanny. When Imlay lost interest in their relationship she became deeply depressed and twice attempted suicide. During this time she travelled through Scandinavia, probably on a business assignment for Imlay, who was the unnamed addressee of a series of letters later published as *A Short Residence in Sweden*. This is more pragmatic and reflective than *A Vindication of the Rights of Woman*, less optimistic in its claims, but also communicating a sense of wisdom and compassion that makes it a more mature work. Wollstonecraft's quest for meaning led her to seek out the connections and resonances in all her experiences and ideas, so that the power of reason is never allowed to silence her feelings of inconsistency, failure and sadness, but neither are the latter allowed to wriggle free of the scrutiny of a rational and searching mind. There is a lyrical, maternal romanticism to her later writing, suggesting a philosophical vision that anticipates the quest of some modern feminists for a style and ethos associated not with the autonomous man of reason but with the maternal self, a person whose identity is constituted through a sense of connection with nature and of bodily interaction with and care for another. In a passage reflecting on a sleepless night during her travels, Wollstonecraft writes:

> I contemplated all nature at rest; the rocks, even grown darker in their appearance, looked as if they partook of the general repose, and reclined more heavily on their foundation. – What, I exclaimed, is this active principle which keeps me still awake? – Why fly my thoughts abroad when every thing around me appears at home? My child was sleeping with equal calmness – innocent and sweet as the closing flowers. – Some recollections, attached to the idea of home,

mingled with reflections respecting the state of society I had been contemplating that evening, made a tear
drop on the rosy cheek I had just kissed; and emotions
that trembled on the brink of extacy [*sic*] and agony
gave a poignancy to my sensations, which made me
feel more alive than usual.

What are these imperious sympathies? How frequently has melancholy and even mysanthropy taken
possession of me, when the world has disgusted me,
and friends have proved unkind. I have then considered myself as a particle broken off from the grand
mass of mankind; – I was alone, till some involuntary
sympathetic emotion, like the attraction of adhesion,
made me feel that I was still a part of a mighty whole,
from which I could not sever myself – not, perhaps, for
the reflection has been carried very far, by snapping
the thread of an existence which loses its charms in
proportion as the cruel experience of life stops or poi-
sons the current of the heart. Futurity, what hast thou
not to give to those who know that there is such a
thing as happiness! I speak not of philosophical con-
tentment, though pain has afforded them the
strongest conviction of it.[3]

This lengthy quotation suggests something of the interweaving of emotion and reflection, sentimentality and
grief, a mother's love and a lover's loss, a deep delight in
nature and a suicidal sense of forsakenness, that inform
Wollstonecraft's writings. For some, this stylistic extrava-
gance makes her philosophy the poorer, but it is arguably
an attempt to reason from the depths of the heart.

Just before the Second World War, de Beauvoir wrote:

Little by little I had abandoned the quasi-solipsism and
illusionary autonomy I cherished as a girl of twenty;

though I had come to recognise the fact of other people's existence, it was still my individual relationships with separate people that mattered most to me, and I still yearned fiercely for freedom. Then suddenly, History burst over me, and I dissolved into fragments. I woke to find myself scattered over the four corners of the globe, linked by every nerve in me to each and every other individual.[4]

Just as Wollstonecraft's thought resists the idea of the isolated individual and affirms an inseparable sense of being 'part of a mighty whole', de Beauvoir too felt herself 'linked by every nerve' to others.

The psychologist Carol Gilligan, in her study of the moral development of men and women, suggests that from the time of adolescence, women's moral values tend to be directed towards the imperative to preserve relationships and care for others, while men's values tend to be more concerned with defending principles of justice and respecting the autonomy of others. Gilligan refers to 'two ways of speaking about moral problems, two modes of describing the relationship between other and self'.[5] She suggests that women tend to represent relationships in web-like imagery, while men use more hierarchical images. But in societies dominated by masculine values, Gilligan argues that women learn not to trust their own perceptions and judgements, because they are seen as less focused and clear-thinking than men. This has the effect of silencing women's voices, because a lack of confidence in their moral judgements translates into a sense of personal inadequacy and failure. Only when society learns to value both these patterns of thought and to integrate them into a more complete moral vision, does Gilligan see a way beyond the sexual inequalities and ethical failures of the present social order. She writes:

There have been two strands to the western moral tradition. One focuses on contract, on enlightened self-
interest, and on the extension to the other of the
rights and claims that are one's own. This might be
called a self-interested form of morality, and it is tied
to the notion of social contract in its modern formulation. The second tradition is that of self-sacrifice,
which is tied to the notion of altruism. For centuries,
these two lines of morality have wandered through the
western traditions, appearing in the contrast between
reason and compassion, fairness and forgiveness, justice and mercy, and emerging repeatedly, although by
no means exclusively, in the contrast between men
and women ...

Listening to women talk about moral conflict and choice,
and about themselves in relation to others, I have observed
that women tend to translate the abstract language of
moral discourse into the vernacular of human relationships. This is usually grounds for criticizing women's
moral thinking, i.e. for saying that women confuse moral
problems with problems of interpersonal relationships. But
the very 'confusion' is revealing. The two moral languages,
of self-interest and self-sacrifice, came to be labelled as
'selfish' and 'selfless' by women ... And the criticism of
these two words, indeed a criticism of the very polarity of
self-interest and self-sacrifice, is that they both exclude
relationship. Selfish means excluding the other, and selfless
implies excluding the self, which creates a special problem
with moral choice, since there is then no self, actor, or
agent in the situation of choice. In any case, both
selfishness and selflessness imply an exclusion which
destroys relationships. There is no relationship if others
are not present in their own terms, or if the self is
silenced.6

I shall return to these ideas, for they point to the importance, not only of listening to what women say, but of knowing how to listen with a different set of questions and
values. If we measure women like Wollstonecraft and de
Beauvoir against the language and values of masculine
philosophy, they will seem less clear in their arguments,
less direct in their principles, and less focused in their
visions. But if we recognise that such women are thinking
from within the midst of human relationships, that their
philosophical reflections are inextricably interwoven with
the demands of care and of preserving even painful and
inadequate relationships, such as that between Wollstonecraft and Imlay or, arguably, between de Beauvoir and
Sartre, then perhaps we will find a different voice in which
to give collective expression to the values that women stand
by and stand for, in the interests of developing a more integrated and holistic moral vision in which both men and
women can become rounded human beings.

On her return to England, Wollstonecraft began a love
affair with Godwin and conceived her second daughter, the
future Mary Shelley. She married Godwin in 1797, perhaps
believing that she had at last achieved something close to
her vision of an ideal marriage based on friendship, equality and mutual respect. She died six months later at the
age of thirty-eight, ten days after giving birth to Mary.
Godwin published what was at the time a highly contro-
versial biography of Wollstonecraft, *Memoirs of the Author
of 'The Rights of Woman'*, during a period of deep mourning after her death.

Wollstonecraft has, to date, attracted more attention
from secular feminists than from feminist theologians.[7]
However, her writings are threaded through with themes
of theological reflection, making her work a resource for
the reconstruction of a theology of woman that is informed
by the beliefs and questions of women themselves. Like

many Christian women today, Wollstonecraft was disillu-
sioned and impatient with the moralizing platitudes of
institutionalized Christianity, but she also recognized the
radical potential of the Christian faith if it was allowed to
challenge rather than conform to the status quo. Unlike
some feminist theologians, Wollstonecraft did not perceive
any contradiction in a faith that was both rational and radical. On the contrary, she was suspicious of the sentimentality of a faith that appeals only to the emotions, because
she thought it silences the voice of justice. She argues that
'A blind unsettled affection may, like human passions,
occupy the mind and warm the heart, whilst to do justice,
love mercy, and walk humbly with our God, is forgotten.'[8]
But she also insists that 'it is not against strong, persever-
ing passions, but romantic wavering feelings, that I wish to
guard the female heart by exercising the understanding'.[9]

   Anticipating Marx's critique of religion perhaps,
Wollstonecraft claims that 'Men will not become moral
when they only build air castles in a future world to com-
pensate for the disappointments which they meet with in
this', and she goes on to suggest a fundamental incompati-
bility between Christianity and the accumulation of wealth:

> Most prospects in life are marred by the shuffling
> worldly wisdom of men, who, forgetting that they can-
> not serve God and mammon, endeavour to blend con-
> tradictory things. If you wish to make your son rich,
> pursue one course – if you are only anxious to make
> him virtuous, you must take another; but do not imag-
> ine that you can bound from one road to the other
> without losing your way.[10]

In adopting the slogan, 'We believe in life before death',
Christian Aid today echoes Wollstonecraft's belief that
only a faith that is rooted in the material realities of this

life, with all its social and economic demands for justice, is credible. Liberation theology has since the early 1970s been an increasingly diverse but persistent voice that insists upon the social and political dimensions of the Christian faith. For many European Christians, with fresh memories of the ways in which Christianity has been co-opted into the service of ideologies and regimes that have militated against human freedom, this politicization of faith is not to be welcomed unambiguously. But liberation theologians argue that the Church's emphasis on personal piety and sexual morality at the expense of social justice is an indictment of western Christianity, which has colluded in imperialism and capitalism through its failure to challenge economic and political structures which bring death, not life, to the poor. When Wollstonecraft exclaims that 'It is justice, not charity, that is wanting in the world!'[11] she shares this sense of outrage over a sentimentalized and de-politicized morality: 'I have always been an enemy to what is termed charity, because timid bigots endeavouring thus to cover their *sins*, do violence to justice, till, acting the demi-god, they forget that they are men.'[12]

But if Wollstonecraft's social awareness strikes a chord with some contemporary Christian movements, the other aspect of her theology that has relevance today is her recognition that if women are to challenge the injustice of men's laws and social constructs, then they must have recourse to some higher source of justice. Wollstonecraft's concept of reason was rooted in her faith in the absolute justice of God made manifest in the laws of nature. If human reason is warped by men's abuse of power and exploitation of women, then divine reason is a source of greater justice to which women can appeal. 'Nature, or, to speak with strict propriety, God, has made all things right; but man has sought him out many inventions to mar the work.'[13]

The theism of Enlightenment philosophers, notably

that of Kant, posits the idea of God as a rational necessity rather than as a personal and loving deity. But while Wollstonecraft's concept of divinity shares some of these theistic characteristics, it is closer to the Christian idea of God than to the God of the philosophers. She uses the language of love and worship as well as reason in her attempt to express the infinite harmony of virtues that she associates with the divine, as the quotation at the beginning of this chapter suggests.

The wisdom of God is a recurring theme in Wollstonecraft's writings, and she represents it as a characteristic that brings God's power into harmony with all the other characteristics of the divine. She implies that a one-sided emphasis on God's omnipotence is protected by a bogus piety that masks the connection between oppressive forms of human power and a distorted theology. In refusing to interrogate their theology, men were also refusing to interrogate their own relationship to power, whereas contemplation on the wisdom and justice of God challenges the tyranny of divinely sanctioned abusive power.

Feminist theologians point to the ways in which a theology that identifies God with omnipotent masculinity is an ideological construct closely associated with patriarchal power structures. In the words of Mary Daly, 'If God is male, then the male is God.'[14] Grace Jantzen, in her witty feminist deconstruction of Richard Swinburne's theism, writes of his 'implied identification of God with a disembodied omnipotent spirit, the idea that anyone who can imagine "himself" as an infinitely extended (and disembodied) version of an Oxford professor is an analogue of the divine.'[15] From a somewhat different perspective, African women theologians argue that Christian images of power and conquest are closely associated with imperialism and colonialism. Teresa Hinga writes,

During the period of colonial and imperial expansionism, the prevailing image of Christ was that of Christ the conqueror. Jesus was the warrior King, in whose name and banner (the cross) new territories, both physical and spiritual, would be fought for, annexed, and subjugated. An imperial Christianity thus had an imperial Christ to match.[16]

While these contemporary women's voices arise in very different social contexts from that of Wollstonecraft, there is a continuum between her ideas and theirs, in so far as all recognize the corrupting potential of an overemphasis on divine omnipotence, when it is allied to human institutions and power structures. But is faith in the power of God necessarily harmful, or does it also have creative potential in our quest for justice?

The idea of power is often treated with contempt by feminist thinkers, who see it as closely associated with relationships of domination. The term 'empowerment' is sometimes used instead to describe forms of power that are co-operative rather than coercive, based not on hierarchical control but on mutual endeavour and interaction. Thus 'power' comes to be associated with masculine tendencies such as competitiveness, authoritarianism and violence, while 'empowerment' suggests feminine models of co-operation, equality and non-violence. Yet however attractive such a hypothesis might be, it risks a certain naivety about the complex and concealed ways in which power operates in personal and social relationships, for women no less than for men. During the last century, critical theorists have used the insights of Marx and Freud to analyse how modern capitalist societies function in terms of veiled relationships of domination and exploitation, and feminist thinkers have introduced a gendered dimension to these various forms of psychoanalytic and economic analysis. Although

they work from different theoretical perspectives, these
scholars tend to agree that, individually and collectively,
our identities, relationships and social structures are perpetuated and sustained through the intricate and often hidden dynamics of power at work in language and in cultural
institutions, so that it is almost impossible to escape the
coercive and abusive effects of power. At best, one can be
attentive to the risks associated with power, and resolve to
recognize and resist its seductive or debilitating effects.

Like all movements that have preceded it, feminism
must address the question of its own relationship to power,
particularly with regard to the tension between the liberal
emphasis on freedom of choice and autonomy, and the
social responsibility to limit one's freedom and forego certain choices in the interests of one's social and moral
duties to others. Much popular feminism has uncritically
embraced the values of a liberal consumerist society that
sees choice not as a means to an end but as an end in itself,
so that the illusion of freedom that is implied in the word
'choice' distracts from deeper issues concerning not only
what women are free from, but just as importantly, what
women are free for.

Since the emergence of modern feminism in the late
1960s, a multiplicity of feminisms has developed in the
recognition that early feminism was informed primarily by
the concerns and ambitions of white, middle class western
women. While many women outside this relatively privileged minority recognize the liberating potential of feminism, they also see a need to explore forms of feminism
that are not subservient to liberal western interests. At the
fourth UN conference on women in Beijing in 1995, some
Third World delegates argued that the agenda was dominated by western women's demands, while ignoring urgent
issues of poverty, health care and education in the world's
poorer nations. This ongoing debate between so-called

First World and Third World feminists suggests something of what is at stake when feminism becomes another political ideology vying for supremacy in a global environment dominated by the richest nations. It also raises questions about the relationship between feminism and the secular liberal worldview that began to take shape in western culture at the time of the Enlightenment.

One of the premises of the Enlightenment and the revolutions that followed in western politics and culture was that authority must be earned and freely conferred if our political hierarchies and institutions are to avoid the exercise of tyrannical power. This is the bedrock of democracy, and it is a vision that continues to reverberate, perhaps more universally today than ever before, as campaigners around the world appeal to principles of democracy and human rights to resist dictatorial regimes and corrupt forms of government. There are thinkers who see this universalization of human rights as yet another form of imperialism, with the values and beliefs of an inherently western, Judaeo-Christian worldview being imposed on other cultures and religions, in a way that makes them compliant with the hegemony of western political and economic interests. Even for those of us who would defend the human rights movement against such charges, it is hard to deny that there is something deeply contradictory about the globalization of the free market and the militarization of western economies such as Britain and America with their heavy investment in the arms trade and defence spending, and the claim that these are motivated by essentially humanitarian concerns to protect and promote freedom and democracy. These issues suggest something of the complexity of power, its uses and abuses, whether in personal relationships or in the international order. Without some form of power, it is impossible for individuals or communities to achieve their goals, but the acquisition

of power so often brings with it the corruption of ideals.
Wollstonecraft experienced this firsthand in the Terror of
the French Revolution. Across Africa, visionaries who
fought for the freedom of their people became the new
tyrants of the postcolonial era, inflicting on their peoples
forms of oppression and suffering that sometimes exceeded
those of their former imperial conquerors.

One of the problems with oversimplifying issues of
power and domination is that it can lead to the romanti-
cization of the oppressed, in such a way that oppressors and
oppressed are portrayed as two radically different groups of
people, rather than as individuals who negotiate shifting
positions of strength or weakness, mastery or subservience,
between and within the myriad relationships that constitute our communal environments. Those who are the most
powerless of all in the social or economic order usually find
somebody weaker or more marginalized to lord it over. For
the poor and emasculated man, this might be his wife or
children. For the downtrodden woman, it might be her own
daughter or daughter-in-law or some other close family
relation. It is the rare and saintly individual who manages
to rise above all such prejudices and violences, and it is only
the weakest and most vulnerable person who can escape
them altogether. Wollstonecraft herself saw that women
have not simply been the victims of history but have also,
from a position of apparent powerlessness, sometimes exercised particularly manipulative forms of power over those
weaker than themselves. She writes that woman 'has
always been either a slave or a despot'.[17]

The American political theorist, Jean Bethke Elshtain,
argues that, historically, women have lacked the institutionalized power – *potestas* – that constitutes the power of
the law, the social order and public life. But she sees
women as wielding a different kind of power – *potentia* –
which is a form of charismatic, personal influence that, like

potestas, can be used for good or for ill. It can be expressed as a manipulative, coercive form of power, but it can also be used to subvert the dominance of *potestas* in the interest of care and compassion for the weak and the vulnerable. She writes,

> Women, in and through their powerlessness, understand what it means to be vulnerable. Their openness to beginnings, even under conditions of hardship and privation, terror and torture, has daily renewed the world, making possible future beginnings. The challenge for women at this fateful juncture is to keep alive memories of vulnerability as they struggle to overcome structurally sanctioned inefficacy and to reaffirm rather than repudiate interdependencies as they seek a measure of institutional 'legitimacy'. Women, from a double position that straddles powerlessness and power, are in a powerful position to insist with Albert Camus that one must never avert one's eyes from the suffering of children and, seeing that suffering, one is required to act.[18]

But this is where the question of divine power becomes significant, since it has the potential to relativize as well as to absolutize human power. As Wollstonecraft implies and many contemporary feminists argue, there is a demonstrable connection between Christian theology, with its emphasis on an omnipotent and omniscient masculine deity, and forms of social organization that give men power over women, and that privilege characteristics associated with masculinity over those associated with femininity. There is an almost unbroken link between Greek philosophical concepts and Christian theological arguments that have continued to identify men with divinity, reason and authority, and women with animality, emotion and submission. Given the ample evidence that men have used the idea of God to validate their power over women in the Christian social order, it is understandable that many feminists today are particularly wary of those who appeal to Christianity as a source of justice and truth about the human condition. It is not easy to defend the Church against such criticisms when male church leaders, particularly those in the Roman Catholic hierarchy, expend so much energy on defining and controlling the place of women. But to acknowledge these manifold difficulties and the ways in which the Christian perception of divine power has often been a barely masked ideology of male domination, is only part of the Christian story. It must be balanced by a recognition of the ways in which faith in the power and justice of God can also set limits to human power, and provide a court of appeal beyond the laws of human institutions.

The failure of many secular visions and institutions invites a reconsideraton of divine presence and power, but from a new perspective. If Christianity has often failed women in the past, the same is true of the philosophical, political and scientific institutions of the post-Christian world. Indeed, Elshtain suggests that the emergence of the secular liberal tradition had the effect of a radical silencing of women's voices by depriving the private sphere of moral worth, and investing in a value system that saw only one form of language – the scientific discourse of rationalism – as having any collective significance. Referring to philosophers such as Robert Filmer, Thomas Hobbes and John Locke, she argues that

> By failing to come up with a vocabulary rich enough to account for the centrality of the social relationships of the family, even as they 'depoliticized' these relationships, thinkers within the liberal tradition adopted a set of assumptions which required the 'systematic

setting to one side of the fundamental facts of birth, childhood, parenthood, old age, and death'.[19]

The consequence is that 'The human subject is deprived of the power of individual speech: a *potentia* destroyed by the external imposition of an absolute power, *potestatis*.'[20] Women, long associated with the discourse of the private realm, suffered from a particularly acute form of silencing in this transition to modernity. But, suggests Elshtain, as women now begin to emerge from the silence of the private world to which they were consigned, an important question arises: 'Having begun to enter the public world in large numbers the debate, for women, is: under what terms does this public activity occur? Can the traditional concerns of women in the private realm "speak" to the public world? Should they? How?'[21]

Gilligan's response to such questions is that women need 'a different voice' in which to speak and be heard. Both Elshtain and Gilligan agree that public life and moral values are diminished when the sphere of women's concerns – the domestic world of relationships of care, nurture and compassion – is deprived of its value and significance in the ordering of society. For Elshtain, this devaluation of the relational dimensions of morality and language can be traced back to the beginnings of the secular modern worldview.

Women have played little part in the ideological struggles of the past, and only in the late twentieth century has there been a collective women's voice capable of challenging men's assumptions about God, human values and the social order. That means that women can reopen the question of God, to ask if there might be a new theological vision and indeed a new language – 'a different voice' – latent in women's religious experiences and longings, that can take us beyond both the historical domination of men's religious power and the barrenness of secular materialism,

to a new understanding of our personal and social potential as creatures made in the image of God.

It is with this in mind that I want to reconsider the
Christian idea of God, from the perspective of the questions that women ask about who we are and who we might
become. But before doing that, I want to first consider the
popular image of women in our postmodern society, at the
beginning of the third millennium. Who are we? What have
we become? Where are we going?

1   Mary Wollstonecraft, *A Vindication of the Rights of Woman* [1792] (London:
    Penguin Books, 1992), p. 134.
2   Mary Wollstonecraft, A Short Residence in Sweden [1796] in Mary
    Wollstonecraft and William Godwin, *A Short Residence in Sweden and
    Memoirs of the Author of 'The Rights of Woman'* [1798], Richard Holmes (ed.)
    (London: Penguin Books, 1987), p. 171.
3   Wollstonecraft, *Short Residence*, pp. 69–70.
4   Simone de Beauvoir, *The Prime of Life*, trans. Peter Green (Harmondsworth:
    Penguin, 1965), p. 369.
5   Carol Gilligan, *In a Different Voice: Psychological Theory and Women's
    Development* (Cambridge, MA and London: Harvard University Press, 1993), p.
    1.
6   Carol Gilligan, 'A Different Voice in Moral Decisions' in Diana L. Eck and
    Devaki Jain (eds.), *Speaking of Faith: Cross-cultural Perspectives on Women,
    Religion and Social Change* (London: The Women's Press, 1986), pp. 225–6.
7   Ann Loades is one of the few feminist theologians to engage with
    Wollstonecraft. See Ann Loades, *Feminist Theology: Voices from the Past*
    (Cambridge: Polity Press; Malden, MA: Blackwell Publishers, 2001).
8   Wollstonecraft, *Vindication*, p. 135.
9   Ibid., p. 171.
10 Ibid., p. 222.
11 Ibid., p. 167.
12 Wollstonecraft, *Short Residence,* p. 187.
13 Wollstonecraft, *Vindication*, p. 113.
14 Mary Daly, *Beyond God the Father: Towards a Philosophy of Women's
    Liberation* (London: The Women's Press, 1986), p. 19.
15 Grace Jantzen, *Becoming Divine: Towards a Feminist Philosophy of Religion*
    (Manchester: Manchester University Press, 1998), p. 28.
16 Teresa M. Hinga, 'Jesus Christ and the Liberation of Women' in Mercy Amba
    Oduyoye and Musimbi R. A. Kanyoro (eds.), *The Will to Arise: Women,
    Tradition, and the Church in Africa* (Maryknoll, NY: Orbis Books, 1992), p. 187.

[17] Wollstonecraft, *Vindication*, p. 145.

[18] Jean Bethke Elshtain, 'The Power and Powerlessness of Women' in Gisela Bock and Susan James (eds.), *Beyond Equality and Difference: Citizenship, Feminist Politics and Female Subjectivity* (London and New York: Routledge, 1992), p. 122.

[19] Jean Bethke Elshtain, *Public Man, Private Woman*, 2nd edn (Princeton, NJ: Princeton University Press, 1993), p. 107, quoting Robert Paul Wolff, 'There's Nobody Here But Us Persons' in Carol Gould and Marx Wartofsky (eds.), *Women and Philosophy* (New York: G.P. Putnam, 1976), p. 133.

[20] Elshtain, *Public Man, Private Woman*, p. 114.

[21] Ibid., p. 114.

2
Cosmo Girl and the Death of God

'Why I'll always be a *Cosmo* Girl'
Imogen Edwards-Jones, aged thirty-three[1]

Have you not heard of that madman who lit a lantern in the bright morning hours, ran to the market-place and cried incessantly: 'I am looking for God! I am looking for God!' – As many of those who did not believe in God were standing together there he excited considerable laughter. Have you lost him then? said one. Did he lose his way like a child? said another. Or is he hiding? Is he afraid of us? Has he gone on a voyage? Or emigrated? – thus they shouted and laughed. The madman sprang into their midst and pierced them with his glances. 'Where has God gone?' he cried. 'I shall tell you. We have killed him – you and I. We are all his murderers. But how have we done this? How were we able to drink up the sea? Who gave us the sponge to wipe away the entire horizon? What did we do when we unchained this earth from its sun? Whither is it moving now? Whither are we moving now? Away from all suns? Are we not perpetually falling? Backward, sideward, forward, in all directions? Is there any up or down left? Are we not straying as through an infinite nothing? Do we not feel the breath of empty space? Has it not become colder? Is more and more night not coming on all the time? Must not lanterns be lit in the morning? Do we not hear anything yet of the noise of the gravediggers who are burying God? Do we not smell anything yet of God's decomposition? – gods, too, decompose. God is dead. God remains dead. And we have killed him. How shall we, the murderers of all murderers, console ourselves?

Friedrich Nietzsche, 1844–1900[2]

For the philosophers of the Enlightenment, including
Mary Wollstonecraft, the moral universe was held together
and made meaningful by God, although this rational and
impersonal deity differed in significant ways from the
personal, incarnate God of the Christian faith. Enlightenment thinkers believed that human beings were made in
the image of God by virtue of being creatures of reason, but
like Eve, faced with what they perceived as a choice
between the knowledge of good and evil and unquestioning
obedience to God, they chose the former. Human freedom
made it necessary that one was morally obliged to follow
the laws of reason rather than the dictates of faith.

After a century in which medieval Christendom had
fragmented into warring factions and rivalrous doctrines,
when the Catholic worldview had buckled under the pressure not only of its own internal abuses of power, but also
of a growing spirit of individualism and rationalism in
western culture, obedience to a God who seemed to collude
in the tyranny of kings and clerics, and in whose name so
many acts of violence and injustice were perpetrated, was
increasingly problematic. The quest began for a new basis
for explaining what it means to be a free and moral human
being. This transition from a medieval to a modern concept
of human subjectivity is often associated with the philosopher Descartes, whose famous claim 'I think, therefore I
am' (*cogito ergo sum*) is seen as the catalyst for the making
of the modern man of reason – sometimes referred to as
the Cartesian 'I'. Although Descartes was a Catholic whose
primary concern in his *Meditations* was to prove not only
his own existence but also God's existence, he articulated
the idea of the autonomous, self-knowing individual that
would profoundly affect the western understanding of
what it means to be human.

The Christian worldview that prevailed until the late
Middle Ages was that of an organic creation, dependent

upon and cared for by its creator. Although the relationship between God and creation had been marred by original sin, the incarnation of God in Christ had restored grace to the universe, and the living world pulsed with the presence of God. Human beings were part of the natural world and shared many of the characteristics of other animals, but we were also unique in all creation because as rational animals we were made in the image of God and called to become divine in Christ. God was revealed supremely in the person of Christ but also in the natural world, and thus it was possible to discern truth through the use of reason and the study of the laws of nature. God's laws were written into nature, and reason was the faculty that enabled the human creature to interpret these laws and understand what it means to be good. This idea of natural law entered Christianity through Greek philosophy, and it was given its fullest theological articulation in Thomas Aquinas's reinterpretation of Aristotelian philosophy. As well as reliably being able to know the natural and moral laws that govern the material world and society, human beings could also know something of the nature of God. Although God is an impenetrable mystery, radically beyond all human conceptualization and language (sometimes referred to as the immanent Trinity), God is also self-communicating and self-revealing, made knowable to human consciousness by divine grace active in the scriptures, through the work of the Holy Spirit and in the person of Jesus Christ (this is sometimes called the economic Trinity). Thus while our knowledge of God is limited, we can nevertheless speak meaningfully about God to the extent that God reveals God's self to us.

The self-revelation of God in the natural world through grace was believed to be given its fullest and most truthful expression in the life of the Church. Here, baptized human beings were creatures of a new creation, sacramentally united in and nourished by the maternal body of the Church, acting out the drama of salvation in anticipation of the redemption of the cosmos that was begun in Christ and will be fulfilled at the end of time. This was a communal rather than an individual understanding of what it means to be a person. While our modern concept of subjectivity begins with the self and organizes the world around that core of existence, the medieval concept of self was that of being part of something greater, situated in the world not in terms of his or her own identity but through his or her place in a natural, social and spiritual hierarchy whose meaning was discovered through prayer, ritual and worship, and through the modulated and stratified interactions of the social order.

There is a growing recognition today that the adjective 'medieval' to describe all that is barbaric, superstitious and unenlightened is false. The rich and diverse world of the medieval Church spanned several centuries and stretched across Europe, and if it was an era of crusades, war and persecution, it was also a time of considerable flourishing and social transformation. Nor were women excluded from the positive aspects of medieval society. While they lived in a culture of (sometimes rampant) misogyny and frequent attempts to restrict their freedom, those of the upper classes in particular were able to circumvent the rules and create spaces in which it was possible to have a lasting influence on society and the Church. In every century there are women such as Hilda, abbess of Whitby (d. 680), Hildegard of Bingen (1098–1179), Catherine of Siena (1347–80), Teresa of Avila (1515–82), and Mary Ward (1585–1645), who span the era from the early Middle Ages to the beginning of modernity and who continue to shape Christian spirituality. In the fourteenth century, there were several thousand Beguines living in communities across northern Europe. These were women who lived on the margins of the institutional Church, adopting lifestyles and practising forms of spirituality that expressed something of the dynamic possibilities of the Catholic vision for women when it is not too rigidly fettered by masculine authority figures. The persecution and eventual eradication of these Beguine communities from Catholic life (they had virtually disappeared by the early fifteenth century) point to the power and ruthlessness of the men of the Church in their attempts to control women, but Cathol-icism is arguably unique among all the world's religions in keeping alive the memory and writings of so many women saints and mystics. If a general overview of the premodern world points to sexual inequality and women's oppression by men, the details tell a more complex and nuanced story. The fact that women's historians today can fill in some of these missing details is in no small measure due to the fact that Catholicism has given limited recognition to women's spiritual visions and leadership and preserved a significant body of women's writings, even if this was a selective process that was subject to male legitimation and control.

Although the seventeenth and eighteenth centuries have been seen as a time of growing religious, intellectual and cultural freedoms in western Europe, some scholars question the extent to which these changes were of benefit to women. Like Elshtain, Joan Kelly-Gadol, in her widely quoted article, 'Did Women Have a Renaissance?', argues that the early modern era was a time of diminishing rights for women, when the more rigid separation between the private and public realms deprived them of some of the influence they had enjoyed in feudal societies.[3] While men were carving out a new society based on a radical re-evaluation of human subjectivity and ethics, this did not extend to the sexual sphere. As Wollstonecraft argued so passionately, the great philosophers of the Enlightenment had little interest in starting a sexual revolution.

With the transition from the medieval to the modern worldview, as I suggested above, a new concept of the person emerged. No longer did the western individual understand himself primarily in relation to others, but rather in terms of Kipling's man – self-sufficient, emotionally independent, seeking mastery over himself and the world around him, including the material world associated with nature and with the female body.[4] Protestant Christianity rejected the idea of the Church as a community of salvation, a maternal body constituted by the interdependence of her members and vivified by the sacramental presence of Christ. Salvation became a matter for the individual to work out, and the Bible became the sole source of revelation and authority. Forms of worship were pared down and stripped of their sensuality and sacramentality, in order to focus the mind on the preaching of the Word of God. Thus Christianity began to reflect the new self-consciousness of the modern individual, in a culture in which the body and the natural world were no longer channels of grace and divine revelation, but obstacles to human progress that had to be controlled and subjugated by the rational mind. With the eighteenth century, this became a philosophical rather than a theological vision, and the transition from the medieval to the modern world was more or less complete. Kant argued decisively that, although the facts of God, the immortal soul and freedom must be accepted as *a priori* truths in order to make sense of our human concepts of morality and meaning, nothing more could be said about these metaphysical or noumenal truths. It was only truths that were demonstrable in the empirical world, phenomena that could be observed by the senses and interpreted by reason, that could be meaningfully discovered and discussed. Knowledge would henceforth be a matter not of revelation, prayer and reason, but of reason and science alone. The image of God had begun to blur and fade in the perception of what it means to be human, and today it remains, if at all, as only a lingering watermark around the edges of western consciousness.

If the eighteenth century was an era when God became a philosophical proposition rather than a personal focus of prayer and faith, it was the nineteenth and twentieth centuries that saw the transition from theism to atheism across much of western culture. Nietzsche's proclamation of the death of God gave flamboyant rhetorical expression to a scepticism that was spreading across western societies. Confronted by Darwin's theory of evolution, Freud's discovery of the unconscious, and Marx's analysis of the class struggle, Europe's faith in a distant but still viable God yielded to a new trust in science and reason as the only motivating powers necessary for the advancement of human knowledge and western civilization.

But events of a century that had begun with such confidence seemed to mock this hubristic optimism. Two World Wars exposed the violence that festered in Europe's nation states, and Germany, the cradle of the Enlightenment, showed that science, technology and rationalized bureaucracy could be used in the service of efficient genocide. Out of this chaos emerged a new *zeitgeist*, a postmodernist worldview that has seen the abandonment of any attempt to articulate universal truths, values or beliefs. Parody now takes the place of passion, and meaning has fractured across a myriad of pluralities and relativities. In a post-Holocaust, postcolonial world, many Europeans are afraid of their own power, afraid indeed of their own histories and of the tragedies that they have unleashed in the name of God, progress and civilization. And yet even as we face this collective crisis, we have accumulated power as never before. With the collapse of the Soviet Union and the globalization of the free market economy, with the mushrooming of communications technology and the mass media, there are now few places on earth where human beings can create societies that are not directed and governed by western values, reinforced by the constant threat of economic exclusion and war for those that choose not to conform. The result, perhaps not surprisingly, is a sudden spiralling of violence as so-called terrorists pit themselves against the militarized nation states of the western world, and these nations in turn respond with increasing violence. And where are women in this strange, disordered and fragmented world?

Some feminists, surveying the chaos that men have created, argue that women hold the key to the transformation of values that the world needs today. Women are oriented to life, not death. Our bodies nurture life, and our psyches are formed by the imperative to care, to protect and to relate. Pope John Paul II and some forms of feminism – often referred to as romantic feminism – have much in common in appealing to such arguments. In the encyclical *Evangelium Vitae*, John Paul II calls upon women to promote 'a "new feminism" which rejects the temptation of imitating models of "male domination", in order to acknowledge and affirm the true genius of women in every aspect of the life of society, and overcome all discrimination, violence and exploitation'.[5] In his 'Letter to Women' written in July 1995, he refers to the necessary involvement of women in society, since 'it will force systems to be redesigned in a way which favours the processes of humanisation which mark the "civilisation of love"',[6] a vision that does not, it would seem, extend to the public life and institutions of the Vatican.

But how realistic is this vision? For much of this book, I want to argue that women do indeed offer different ways of viewing and valuing the living world, and that the exclusion of women from the formation and development of western religious, political and intellectual life has had a detrimental effect on our humanity and our culture. But for now, I want to identify the very real problems and obstacles to this vision, and in order to do this I want to consider what western women have achieved after thirty years of feminism.

In March 2002, the British edition of the best-selling women's magazine *Cosmopolitan* celebrated thirty years of publication. The cover stories for this celebratory issue included 'Cameron Diaz: "Love, Diets & Why I'm Quitting Hollywood for a Year"'; 'Sex in Space, On the Seabed, Up a Mountain – Extreme Orgasms Tried & Tested (Really)!'; '*Cosmo* vs Cellulite: What Works, What Doesn't'; 'Domestic Violence Campaign: The Truth is Out ... 40% of You are Battered Women'. If this is an identikit picture of modern woman, what does it suggest? Somebody who worries about her weight and appearance, is fascinated by Hollywood stars, has improbable sexual fantasies while fretting about her sexual performance, and is quite possibly being beaten and abused by the man she shares her home with.

The journalist Katherine Viner offers a critical assessment of feminism in an article in the *Guardian* newspaper. She sees a worrying trend in which consumerism has taken the place of feminist activism and radicalism, so that from the market in pornography to the cosmetics industry, women have been seduced into exchanging hard-won freedoms for 'women's lib by credit card'. Referring to contemporary marketing techniques, she writes, 'you are not just purchasing something, you are engaging with it personally, so that you will feel better – and be a better person – just by having it. And that applies to cars as much as it does to porn. ... Shopping itself has been fetishised into women's greatest pleasure, and the most empowering thing you can do for yourself is to go to a beauty therapist.'[7] One need only think of the advertising slogan used by the cosmetic firm, *L'Oréal* – 'Because you're worth it' – to see the truth in this.

But consumerism feeds on insatiable demand. Viner points to the influence of Edward Bernays, founding father of public relations, in recognizing the commercial potential of Freudian desire. While both Christian theology and post-Enlightenment philosophy have tended to view desire with suspicion, consumerism has unleashed it from the controls of reason and virtue, and made it a driving force behind the modern social order. In the aftermath of September 11, 2001, both George W. Bush and Tony Blair expressed concern that the effects of that catastrophe would damage consumer confidence. We were urged not to let the terrorists win, by continuing to shop. It never seemed to occur to our leaders that perhaps reluctance to go shopping was because, in the face of such enormous events, shopping loses its escapist potential. Confronted with the most profound questions of evil, suffering, violence, justice and courage, we might have seen our consumerist culture for what it is and turned our backs on it. And of course, few politicians sought to ask if there might be some deep connection between our consumer economy, and the despairing violence of those who are culturally, politically, religiously and economically excluded from these collective forms of illusion and escapism. In Spike Lee's film *Malcolm X*, there is the line, 'The most dangerous person in the world is the one with nothing to lose.' September 11, 2001, was chilling evidence of what that can mean, and the more we create a world where a few have everything to hold onto and many millions have nothing to lose, the more dangerous that world will become.

Women in the western democracies have yet to become an alternative political force capable of challenging this situation, despite nearly a century of universal suffrage. Of course, there are many individuals and women's groups who do indeed struggle to create a new social vision, but by and large the early feminist ideal of an international collective of women bound together by a sense of sisterhood simply by virtue of their sex seems impossibly naive and optimistic. If women are to bring about the kind of social, moral and economic transformations that might contribute to a different way of being in the world, that is likely to take several generations of determined struggle and hopeful perseverance. In the meantime, it is important to ask if the increased affluence and opportunities of western liberal societies have created a culture of women who are more at peace with themselves, with men and with society. While happiness is impossible to assess objectively, the majority of modern women do not seem to be significantly happier than our predecessors. Certainly, many of us enjoy a level of physical comfort and security of which our grandmothers could only dream. But given the magnitude of the therapy industry, the fretful quest for the perfect partner, the perfect home, the perfect child, the perfect career, the growing number of broken marriages and of impoverished single mothers, the increasing sexual commodification and exploitation of women and children, and the rise in alcoholism, drug addiction and crime among women, it is clear that the material and social gains of recent decades have at best been a mixed blessing. We are left with Freud's question: 'What does a woman want?'

A browse through that issue of *Cosmopolitan* reinforces the idea of modern womanhood as being in a state of rootlessness and restlessness, a vacuous and incoherent parodying of the worst characteristics that men have attributed to women through the ages – frivolous, sexually wanton, vain and profligate. The articles and advertisements all represent sex as a performance, a masquerade, a competition even, when women must go to ever greater and more extreme lengths to please their men – while pretending that they are also pleasing themselves. 'Before we know it, she's [Danni Minogue] revealed all her sexy secrets – from the hotspots that make her melt to why she fancies Dermot O'Leary and why female ejaculation is important!' The interview with Danni Minogue reveals that her parents 'are still married and in love and they're an almost-extinct species'. In another article, 'Sara' explains that 'In the half an hour we were underwater we managed three sexual positions. They were all great although Shawn did hurt me when we had sex while I was on my back.' Meanwhile, Laura, who had sex with Jules on the top of a mountain in the Alps, 'had a really intense orgasm' and would 'recommend sex up a mountain'. Who is she kidding?

Elsewhere though, a different perspective emerges. One article is entitled 'My Boyfriend Raped Me In His Sleep.' In another, *EastEnders* actress Kacey Ainsworth describes what it was like to play a scene in which her character, Mo, was beaten by her husband Trevor: 'Even though I'm an actress, at that point when I was on the floor, I felt totally and utterly humiliated and sick. I felt Little Mo's degradation at having her head shoved into a plate of food. What was more frightening was I knew this scene could have been real, that it's all part of the power game these men play to make women feel as if they're worthless.'

Thus *Cosmopolitan* tries to inject a slice of social realism into its fantasy world. On the page opposite the above quotation, there's a full-page advertisement showing a woman's perfect, scantily-clad posterior: 'Contour + Tone Shape Up Your Body!'

My point is that magazines like these are actually part of the power game, part of the hidden tactical manoeuvres that go on in our supposedly free and equal societies 'to make women feel as if they're worthless'. Insatiable desire feeds on inconsolable loss, and thus society no longer needs laws, religious taboos and social conventions to keep women compliant as it did in Wollstonecraft's time. It only needs an advertising and media industry that reinforces to women at every point the message of how inadequate and lacking we are, and therefore how much we need to change, how many products, clothes and accessories we need to buy, in order to become acceptable to society by being attractive to men.

When Rousseau said that 'man is born free and everywhere he is in chains', he was referring to our inability to sustain a state of perfect liberty, and our willingness to bind ourselves to rules that restrict our freedom in order to form societies. It has taken no time at all for women to exchange a precarious and emergent freedom for the chains that have always bound women, in order to keep the existing social order more or less intact. When Wollstonecraft accused Rousseau of lasciviousness, it was because he saw a wife's primary duty as that of remaining sexually pleasing for her husband. 'The woman who has only been taught to please will soon find that her charms are oblique sunbeams, and that they cannot have much effect on her husband's heart when they are seen every day, when the summer is passed and gone',[8] scoffed Wollstonecraft. Today, it is not just their husbands but men in general, all men everywhere, that women must attract, by conforming to some impossible and cruel ideal of physical perfection and sexual performance that feeds a restless, voracious appetite for more of everything, because nothing in the end brings the satisfaction and success that the package promised. Beneath the glossy smile of *Cosmo* girl lurks a muffled cry of distress and alienation.

That issue of *Cosmopolitan* includes an article by its longstanding agony aunt Irma Kurtz, 'Irma's Agony Years'. After surveying the changing concerns of women over three decades, she concludes as follows:

Of all the agony that has come my way there is one eternally asked question that I hope (hopelessly) never ever to hear again. 'He doesn't like my friends/he can't get it up/he never says he loves me,' writes the modern girl as her foremothers before her.

'Sort him out,' I tell her, 'ease him into it, teach him to know better. Or find somebody who does what your current partner won't or cannot do.' Then I read on, and too often the woman of this new century echoes the female line before: 'What's wrong with me?' 'Nothing is wrong with you,' I want to scream. 'Nothing! Tell him to drop me a line. You are the greatest, the best. Just like *Cosmo*, you are better than ever!

And just to reinforce this gush of affirmation, the opposite page bears a full-size advertisement of another impossibly perfect female body clad in impossibly expensive lace underwear. 'I might raise the temperature a little.' This visual image contradicts Kurtz's message, for it says, far more powerfully, that what this failed woman really needs to do is to have a body overhaul, buy a lace bra, and create a bordello for her man every night.

Kurtz presents sexual relationships in the language of control and commodification. Sort him out or find somebody else. But she also suggests that there is something fundamental about women's desires. Twenty-first century women, like their foremothers, do not want to be made to choose between their friends and their partners. They do not want to be made to feel sexually inadequate. And they want to be loved. Imogen Edward-Jones, browsing through thirty years of past issues, makes the same observation. She writes that 'most striking about these old issues was how little things have changed. Many women are still looking for a man who understands them.'

One response to this kind of observation would be to argue that women are still deeply conditioned by patriarchy to think of themselves only in terms of their relationships to others in general and to men in particular. The solution would be for women to be more independent, more assertive in their demands, and more self-confident in their attitudes – as Kurtz suggests. But even if this is true up to a point, it risks setting up the modern, autonomous individual as the ideal model for both sexes, in a way that seems to deny many of the insights that history, psychology and experience offer in terms of understanding women's desires and subjectivities.

Both Gilligan and Elshtain argue that roles of relating, caring and nurturing are deeply bound up with women's sense of self, and that to deny legitimacy to those roles is to condemn women to silence, or to co-opt them into a society premised entirely upon masculine values and morals. Irigaray puts forward a similar argument. In her critique of de Beauvoir, she suggests that campaigns for women's equality are misguided if they only aspire to equal rights with men. She asks, 'What do women want to be equal to? Men? A wage? A public position? Equal to what? Why not to themselves?'[9]

The women readers of *Cosmopolitan* experience the feelings of inadequacy and failure that Gilligan describes, because they live in a culture that cannot hear what they are saying. Instead of offering a quest for new meanings and values capable of giving authentic voice to women's desires, the glossy magazines have created a cult of womanhood that feeds on a sense of inadequacy and self-alienation, because, just like earlier theological and cultural representations of women in western society, the image they create is based not on a genuine recognition of sexual difference but on a fantasy of woman as man's sexual 'other'. Thus sexuality is not represented as a gift for

receiving and expressing love, but as an achievement by
which a woman becomes valued not for who she is but for
how good she looks and how well she performs. Beauty is
not portrayed as that elusive quality that goes hand in
hand with qualities such as goodness, love and truth, but
as a manufactured commodity that can be packaged and
purchased by those who can afford it. And women's capacity for healthy desire and sexual attraction is replaced by a
narcissistic craving for the perfect self that stifles the
capacity for mature and loving relationships.

For women to go beyond the present impasse, we need
to approach anew the most radical questions about the
meaning and purpose of our lives, but we live in a culture that
actively discourages us from doing this. When we feel those
deep stirrings within us, those ultimate and sometimes
anguished questions that push us towards the horizon not
just of this life but of every life, not just of our own
significance but of every possible significance, we are
advised to seek counselling or therapy. Reflection on the
unavoidable challenge of life's fragility and indeed tragedy
– source of inspiration for all great philosophy, theology, literature and art – has no place in a culture that regards all
suffering as wrong. We might try to find relief by dipping
in and out of books that we buy in the Mind, Body, Spirit
section in our local bookshop, sampling a few religious
ideas without committing ourselves to any of them, looking
for different mechanisms that might scratch the itch. A bit
of yoga, a bit of meditation, maybe even a bit of prayer,
some New Age thoughts, some strategies of self-affirmation and positive thinking. Anything to avoid that dark
space where there is only a wordless question, an unanswerable mystery, not a force but a silent calling that
seems to come from somewhere within that we cannot
identify, and from somewhere beyond the farthest star that
we cannot discover. Who am I? Who are you? To ask these

questions, we need to be able to speak of God, and it is here
that we must begin the quest for a new language and a different voice.

Between the death of Wollstonecraft and the birth of
Cosmo girl, God too died in western culture. Nietzsche pre-
dicted what the death of God would mean, and how com-
placent and unthinking society would be in the face of this
monumental, unprecedented bereavement. For Nietzsche,
the death of Christianity's God created a space for the
emergence of the Superman. Through the will to power,
Nietzsche's ideal man would triumph over Christianity's
legacy that had weakened the human spirit with its
message of servility and humility. By appealing to the symbolic significance of Greek gods such as Apollo and
Dionysus, Nietzsche proclaimed the return of an era based
on the affirmation rather than the negation of human
power, not rooted in the truths of the Christian faith but on
a celebratory acceptance of the futility and nihilism of life.

Although Nietzsche's philosophical vision can arguably
be seen as fuelling a cult of aggressive masculinity, and
indeed he was the favoured philosopher of the Nazis, some
contemporary feminist philosophers such as Daly and
Irigaray see his critique of Christian values and his questioning of western morality as a useful resource for
feminist thought. In a Nietzschean world stripped of essential and absolute truths, it is possible to question even the
most apparently obvious or unchanging meanings.
Irigaray argues that the Nietzschean death of God opens
the way for the rebirthing of the divine, this time not as a
projection of masculine ideals and values, but as a way of
exploring the contours of feminine subjectivity.[10] Daly
adopts a Nietzschean approach in her subversion of
Christian morality, reclaiming the language of female denigration and condemnation to make it a language that
affirms and celebrates female sexuality. On her website she

describes herself as 'a positively revolting hag', and her
philosophy is couched in language that mimics
Christianity's worst caricatures of woman in order to
reclaim and rehabilitate female sexual subjectivity after
two thousand years of Christian repression.[11]

Daly and Irigaray offer extreme but provocative critiques
of Christianity. Although they deal in over-simplifications
and fail to recognize the diversity of the Christian tradition,
their work has inspired many feminist theologians to go
beyond an appeal to women's experience as the basis for a
theology of woman, to an appreciation of the ways in which
our concepts of humanity and divinity, with all their accom-
panying theological, anthropological and moral discourses,
are shaped by language. The metaphors, symbols and
images we use and the ways in which we construct language
not only express but also produce our sense of self. In other
words, we are not the autonomous, self-determining individuals of post-Enlightenment thought. We are inhabitants
of complex cultural and linguistic worlds, and we create
meaning through our engagement with those worlds by way
of conformity or struggle. Robert Burns prayed, 'O that God
the gift would gie' us, to see ourselves as others see us', but
modern critical theory suggests that to a large extent, we are
incapable of seeing ourselves except as others see us. We
have no inner self, untainted or unaffected by others. We
come into a world in which society maps our bodies and feelings according to its values, expectations and rules. For
Freud, this means that our earliest experiences of desire and
loss, sexuality and violence, dependence and alienation, are
hidden even from our own consciousness beneath our culturally conditioned identities. But these repressed and
hidden primal instincts are not an essential or original self,
any more than the self we acquire as we mature is essential
or original. There is no essential 'I', no Kiplingesque man –
or woman – forging an identity out of timeless ideals and

truths innate within us. There is only a struggle of fragmented identities and voices, of powerful drives and fragile
visions doing battle within us as we seek to create a sense
of meaning, a sense of being, against the swirling mysteries
of our own unconscious minds, and of the universe we
inhabit.

If women are to birth new visions of God in this present
crisis of meaning, we can only do so by recognizing the
many ways in which the presence of God has always been
manifested to women through alternative visions of justice, freedom, love and truth that have been able to escape
the limitations and restrictions of a predominantly masculine theological culture. Wollstonecraft's radical critique of
the social order was based not on nihilism, but on faith in
transcendent, divinely inspired values that made life
meaningful. However much reality failed to live up to
those values, she believed that they were true, morally
binding and worth fighting for, because they were vested
not in human behaviour and experience, but in God. It was
God who ensured that ultimately, justice would prevail,
goodness was attainable, love was possible, beyond the
laws and failings of male society. In other words, the power
of God, balanced by love, goodness and compassion, is a
power that works with, not against, women's desires.

For many feminist theologians today, the idea of divine
transcendence and power is antithetical to women's spirituality and experience. Such traditional theological
imagery is equated with an omnipotent, omniscient male
God, set over and against the vulnerability and finitude of
human bodiliness long associated with nature and female
sexuality in western culture. Feminist theologians therefore seek to introduce alternative metaphors and symbols
into theological language – images of a God who is immanent and embodied in creation and the material world, a
God who is maternal, nurturing and vulnerable.[12] Often

this is presented as a new theological vision, although it actually has much in common with some premodern Christian writings. But while feminist theological language can be a necessary corrective to the excessive androcentrism of much modern theology, universal human values can only be defended if they have an objective, transcendent source. God's power relativizes human power, not as a form of tyranny but as a necessary restraint on our otherwise unbridled capacity for domination and exploitation.

When one considers the ways in which Christian women through the ages have perceived and written about God – including Wollstonecraft – it becomes clear that they have seen God not as a tyrannical male deity but as one who sets limits to male power and creates the conditions for female becoming. God has afforded woman a space of freedom beyond the restraints of masculinity for her to explore her own existence in the face of eternity, and while men have tried to colonize and control that space, ultimately women have known that no man controls God. Women have always had to struggle against a vision of self and of God dominated by men's projections and anxieties, and in this respect the writings of the women of the past are often just as problematic as our modern women's magazines in their distorted representations of the female body. But alongside its androcentric theology and institutions, Christianity has also affirmed the ultimate mystery and unknowability of God. This has been the space of female mysticism and spirituality, where women have broken free of the symbols and definitions of men in order to discover new ways of speaking about God and themselves. That this has been an ambivalent exercise fraught with problems I do not deny, and I shall say more about this, but for the vast majority of women in western society, this space of potentially liberating mystery has been cordoned off in the name of reason, autonomy and equality.

The appeal to a just and liberating God is not an option for *Cosmo* girl, because she belongs to a society that is radically and defiantly post-Nietzschean. *Cosmo* girl inhabits a culture that has lost any shared capacity for reflection or any shared quest for meaning, because she inhabits a culture that has forgotten – or silenced – certain ways of talking and certain forms of language. But as a woman who cannot speak about God, *Cosmo* girl cannot speak about herself either. She has no transcendent horizon, no greater power of love that positions her existence and invites her into the fullness of being. This is marketed to her as freedom and self-affirmation, but deep down she knows better. 'What's wrong with me?' 'There's nothing wrong with you,' says the agony aunt, who can appeal to nothing greater than a self mediated through the pages of a glossy magazine to prove her point.

The journalist Cal McCrystal once wrote that 'happiness is the shadow cast by something else'. In the premodern world, Christian morality was understood not in terms of duty, but in terms of happiness. Thomas Aquinas equates the good life with the happy life. It was with thinkers such as Kant that western concepts of morality changed. Being good was about doing one's duty, not about being happy. Kant argues that the only truly moral act is that motivated by a pure sense of duty, uncontaminated by any reward of pleasure. It is little wonder that, faced with such a choice, hedonism has taken the place of happiness in western society, but the problem pages of the glossy magazines and the confessionalism of the media expose the lie that the pursuit of pleasure is the way to happiness. Happiness is the shadow cast by our longing for God, expressed in a sense of neighbourly love and care for the other. In a culture focused on self-gratification, the shadows of alienation and despair deepen around us, and the more we seek to escape the shadows by chasing after one form of purchased pleasure after another, the greater the darkness becomes.

Would the rediscovery of God give modern woman the happiness that eludes her? That is an impossible question to answer, but I do want to suggest that the transformation of self and society depends upon a capacity to discover a transcendent dimension to our lives that can provide a shared language of meaning and a shared vision of goodness. This entails a move beyond the lonely self-sufficiency of our age, to a new discovery of ourselves as creatures who are radically dependent upon loving and being loved. The women who write to *Cosmopolitan* experience this sense of dependence as a source of frustration and self-blame, because it does not sit easily alongside the idea of the independent, self-determining individual that our society values. But thinkers such as Gilligan and Elshtain invite us to recognize the violation of woman's sense of self that this individualism entails, and to find the courage to express a different way of understanding ourselves in relation to others.

As human beings, we come to know who we are only by seeing ourselves as others see us – including God. Time and again, the writings of women saints and mystics, novelists and poets, explore the ways in which a woman can grow into a sense of her own being through living in the gaze of love, just as her sense of self withers when she is not loved and understood. What's wrong with me? Why doesn't he love me? Why doesn't he understand me? Many feminists – myself included – find it difficult to refer to God as 'he', and there is also a tendency to downplay Christ's masculinity because it is used to exclude women from the sacramental life of the Church, including the priesthood. But women's spiritual writings also suggest the idea of God as the ultimate sexual other and the perfect lover, before whose gaze a woman experiences a profoundly erotic calling to discover herself through the freedom that this lover affords.

Consider Catherine of Siena's ecstatic love affair with God. Referring to God as her 'mad lover', she says, 'Why then are you so mad? Because you have fallen in love with what you have made! You are pleased and delighted over her within yourself, as if you were drunk [with desire] for her salvation. She runs away from you and you go looking for her. She strays and you draw closer to her.'[13]

I am not suggesting that contemporary women's spirituality can or should be modelled on the medieval mystics, but in our quest for forms of spirituality that are appropriate to our modern understanding of human psychology and sexuality, there is I believe much that we can learn from women such as Catherine of Siena. I do want to suggest that, in stepping out of the mysterious gaze of God, *Cosmo* girl has not thereby liberated herself. Rather, she has stepped into the pornographic gaze of a media industry fuelled by masculine fantasies and dominated by the corporate greed of its (male) shareholders. Here, the female body becomes inscribed with impossible attributes – wealth, physical perfection, eternal youth, rampant sexuality, assertiveness and power – all designed not to liberate and affirm the female reader, but to fuel her sense of inadequacy, to hold her in bondage to a consumer industry that makes a virtue out of the ancient Christian sins of lust and greed.

So where do we go from here? Does God offer a way beyond this existential crisis? It would be anachronistic to propose a return to traditional Christianity as the solution to the problems of western society, and doubly so for women who until now have been the objects rather than the subjects of theological reflection. In a pluralist culture that encompasses a wide variety of religions and beliefs, it is neither possible nor desirable for Christian theology to reassert itself as a hegemonic discourse of divine revelation and truth. But I believe that for those of us who belong within the Christian tradition, there is a need to situate ourselves in the flux of our postmodern world, with its plurality of cultural and religious narratives, and from that position to think anew – and with confidence – about the promises of the Christian faith and its enduring capacity to inspire great and small acts of love and justice, and to ask how this faith might become once again a living narrative of salvation for women. I believe that it is possible to affirm the dignity of woman made in the image of God from within the Christian tradition, in such a way that what emerges is not a transcendent ideal but a liberating transcendence, experienced in the form of a calling towards the divine in God and in ourselves, a call both to holiness and to wholeness.

1 Imogen Edward-Jones, 'Why I'll Always Be A Cosmo Girl', *Cosmopolitan*, March 2002, p. 159.
2 Friedrich Nietzsche, The Gay Science, in *A Nietzsche Reader*, intro., selection and trans. R.J. Hollingdale (Harmondsworth: Penguin Books, 1977), p. 203.
3 See Joan Kelly-Gadol, 'Did Women Have a Renaissance?' in Renate Bridenthal, Claudia Koonz and Susan Stuard (eds.), *Becoming Visible: Women in European History*, 2nd edn (Boston: Houghton Mifflin, 1987).
4 See Tina Beattie, *Eve's Pilgrimage: A Woman's Quest for the City of God* (London and New York: Burns & Oates, 2002), pp. 119–40.
5. John Paul II, *Evangelium Vitae* (London: Catholic Truth Society, 1995), p. 176, n. 99.
6 John Paul II, 'A Letter to Women', *The Tablet*, 15 July 1995, p. 918.
7 Katherine Viner, 'While We Were Shopping...', The *Guardian*, Wednesday, 5 June 2002 (http://www.guardian.co.uk/Archive/Article/0,4273,4427172,00.html; accessed on 28 June 2002).
8 Wollstonecraft, *Vindication*, pp. 110–1.
9 Luce Irigaray, 'Equal or different?' in Margaret Whitford (ed.), *The Irigaray Reader* (Oxford: Basil Blackwell, 1994), p. 32.
10 See Luce Irigaray, *Sexes and Genealogies*, trans. Gillian C. Gill (New York: Columbia University Press, 1993).
11 See http://www.mdaly.com/; accessed on 2 February 2003; see also Mary Daly, *Outercourse: the Be-dazzling Voyage* (San Francisco: HarperSanFrancisco, 1992).
12 See, for instance, the theology of Sally McFague, including Sally McFague, *The Body of God* (Philadelphia: Augsburg Fortress Publishers, 1993).
13 Catherine of Siena: *The Dialogue*, trans. and introduction by Suzanne Noffke, O.P., preface by Giuliana Cavallini (Mahwah, NJ: Paulist Press, 1980), p. 325.

3
Women, Religion and God

There is one dangerous science for women – one
which let them indeed beware how they profanely
touch – that of theology.

John Ruskin[1]

I have suggested a picture of a confused and confusing
culture, dominated by complacency and apathy, but also
troubled, fragmented, and to some extent lacking in any
real sense of meaning. Reopening the question of God in a
way that is relevant to the meanings that many women
yearn for in this age of crisis is a task that is fraught with
ambiguities and potential pitfalls. It means negotiating a
tangled theological terrain, where a historical tradition of
denigration and blame regarding the place of women in the
Christian story confronts a contemporary culture of often
well-founded scepticism with regard to religion. It also
means recognizing the many ways in which religion continues to be a motivating force in people's lives, despite the
so-called secularism of the age. Indeed, in both its promises and its threats, religion is one of the foremost political
challenges we face at the beginning of the twenty-first
century. Since September 11, 2001, we have been aware
that we face the prospect of spiralling international violence,
perpetuated through the tactics of terror by those who
seek to wage war on the present world order, and by those
who seek to defend it. While we are repeatedly assured that
the West has no quarrel with Islam, nevertheless we have
in recent years witnessed an ongoing war of attrition
between two of the West's most overtly Christian leaders –

George W. Bush and Tony Blair – and the increasingly despairing rage of an alienated and extremist Islamic minority. But it has also become apparent, particularly with regard to America and Britain's war with Iraq, that there is a widening rift between Church and politics concerning the morality of war. While politicians repeatedly invoke the Christian just war tradition to lend legitimacy to their actions, the churches, and in particular the Catholic Church under Pope John Paul II, question whether it is ever possible to fight a just war with the weapons and methods of modern warfare.

This growing sense of disorder and insecurity that confronts us individually and collectively can reinforce a certain rigidity as far as religions are concerned. Religious fundamentalism of all persuasions is a potent force in our modern world because it offers security and certainty, particularly to people who have been denied any other form of security or certainty – a homeland, a decent income, social and political inclusion, an investment in the future. Marx called religion 'the opium of the people' and the 'heart of a heartless world', because he believed it was an ideology that reconciled the oppressed to their suffering through its promise of a better hereafter.

For many women, conformity to religious rules and hierarchies is not a form of enslavement but a way of affirming one's identity and sense of belonging in the face of an increasingly anonymous and impersonal world. Religions tend to value marriage, motherhood and family life more highly than modern secular society, and this can be an attraction for women who derive a strong sense of purpose from their traditional roles. I do not believe that religion is only tolerable for women if it is prised apart from its moorings in patriarchal values. For many women, patriarchy offers a more benign and protective form of social organization than a free market economy. It has established roles for both sexes, with a distribution of rights and responsibilities that is often more effective and fair than feminism recognizes. If, for example, Islam as practised in the contemporary world is often used to control and suppress women, there are also many millions of women for whom Islam provides workable rules and values for the organization of communal and domestic life in the context of obedience to a just and compassionate God. While secular modernity led to the devaluation of domestic and relational values traditionally associated with women's lives, traditional religions continue to insist upon the equal but different significance of these values for the formation of healthy and strong communities. Faced with a choice between conforming to the values of *Cosmo* girl and conforming to the values of a religious tradition, it is by no means obvious why a woman should choose the former over the latter, especially since conformity to the *Cosmopolitan* image presupposes a high level of disposable income. And if modern western women protest that one cannot judge complex realities from images in glossy magazines, religious women could make the same protest. They too are judged far more by media images than by an informed understanding of their lives.

But because religious conservatism often meets profound needs for assurance and a solution to the crisis of alienation in modern society, it does not easily accommodate ambiguity, searching or doubt. It might appear to offer little to attract the restless seeker after truth, the enquiring spirit who takes a precarious gamble on belief. Perhaps that is why feminism is perceived by many religious believers, including many devout women, to be the most threatening of all modern social movements. Feminism calls into question the fundamental beliefs, practices and institutions of the world's religious traditions. It seeks to destabilize human and divine hierarchies that have remained unchanged for centuries, sometimes for millennia. It challenges ancient divisions and boundaries. Women of all religions and none are sometimes united by a vision of women's rights that transcends their religious or cultural differences. Conservatives argue that this is because they have subsumed their faith beneath a western value system that colonizes other beliefs and values and that is therefore the enemy of human diversity and genuine otherness. I think there is some truth in this claim, and it is an issue that calls for vigilance and attentiveness on the part of all those who seek to combine a commitment to women's rights with respect for cultural and religious differences.

However, religious feminism is also marked by a robust plurality, as women scholars and activists struggle to negotiate the difficult terrain between universality and particularity, developing a vision that seeks to affirm our shared humanity while respecting the many ways in which culture, race, religion, sexuality, class and a multitude of other factors interact to create profound differences between human groups and societies. Even if the feminist quest affects only a minority of women, it is still a worldwide, collective movement that can no longer be silenced as it could in Wollstonecraft's time. Women are at the centre of so many of today's social and political upheavals, because as wives, mothers, daughters and sisters, the female sex has until now offered men a more or less stable axis around which to construct their own identities and positions in the world. But now, with more and more women challenging and questioning their roles, men too find themselves cut loose from their moorings, and seeking new ways of building societies and living together. Not surprisingly, there has been a backlash. The Taliban only carried to an extreme the repressive instincts that many conservative churchmen and politicians exhibit when confronted with women's demands for justice. But there are also many men who recognize the need to work with rather than against women in seeking new values to heal our world and offer our children a better future.

That this ongoing revolution is associated with social breakdown and emotional anguish cannot be denied. In Britain today, suicide is a leading cause of death among young men, and we are witnessing a tearing apart of the fabric of society as traditional relationships and values disintegrate in a time of transition between one era and another. It is difficult to know to what extent the change in women's consciousness has contributed to this process, but in my own work with church groups and university students of all ages, I think the impact of feminism should not be underestimated. Among men and women, young and old, there is a profound awareness that something fundamental is shifting around us, and it is associated with the relationship between the sexes. Lectures on feminist theology always bring out deep tensions, anxieties and resistances, as well as affirmations and expressions of hope in the context of lives that are sometimes transformed through this kind of study. Very few people are indifferent to the issues, for they impact upon us at the level of our most intimate relationships as well as in all our social interactions.

In a society organised around masculine values, suffering, violence and death are closely related. For men, suffering is associated with being sick or wounded, and of course with war and aggression. Even when revolutionaries and men of war decide that the suffering associated with violence is a price worth paying to achieve certain objectives, they are still doing a wager with death. But for women, suffering is closely associated with birth as well as with death, and for some of us our most intense experiences of suffering have been those associated with bringing

new life into the world and nurturing that life to maturity.
If childbirth can be – and often is – a struggle that involves
physical agony closely associated with the threat of injury
and death, the vocation to mother the newborn child brings
with it a lifetime of wounded love. Women know that new
life always involves suffering – not the suffering of deliberate violence and aggression, but the inevitable suffering of
being bodily creatures with a capacity to love sometimes
beyond the limits of endurance. Only in this crucible of
hopeful love and creative suffering does new life flourish.

I believe that women can transform the suffering of this
era into a struggle of birthing rather than dying, but that
requires all the wisdom, courage, joy and hope that we can
muster. And it also requires faith – faith in ourselves, faith
in one another and faith in the future, arising out of our
faith in God. God is not an obstacle to the plurality of the
human family and to our longing to find a space of peaceful cohabitation on our beautiful but threatened planet. It
is God who safeguards the space in which human beings
can meet each other on common ground that neither side
controls or owns, providing each agrees that God's transcendence limits human power, that God is mystery
beyond knowing, who invites us to experience our unknowing as a way of reaching out and of asking questions of one
another, of ourselves and of God.

However, if it is ultimately true that God is mystery
beyond all knowing and naming, it is also true that as creatures of language, community and history, we express our
longing for God in the context of religious traditions, each
with its shared symbols and values. To recognize the
mystery of God is not to suggest an abstract God, detached
from and impervious to our human concerns. That is the
God of Enlightenment philosophy, and it is perhaps not
surprising that such a God did not have a very long shelf-
life. Human beings have always been endowed with an

awareness of some transcendent source of life and meaning, which is nevertheless personally involved in the
material world and accessible to human consciousness. For
Freud, that is because God is an oedipal neurosis, an imaginary, infinitely powerful and organizing father figure who
can take the place of our limited and fallible human
fathers. For Ludwig Feuerbach, it is because God is a projection of man's ideals of perfection. For Richard Dawkins,
it is because religion is like a virus in the human system,
that prevents us from recognizing we are nothing other
than very complex gene machines. But none of these theories touches the real question. None of them goes far
enough, nor indeed could any theory ever go far enough, to
explain God, because there would always be a question
more than the one that was answered, born not of science
and psychology but of the complex essence of our humanity with its capacity to imagine the infinite through and
beyond the poetry, beauty, grace and fragility, the comedy,
tragedy, pathos and futility, of this life.

But what kind of God can a woman believe in today? I
have suggested that Wollstonecraft's idea of God as the ultimate source of justice, love and wisdom, who works with
rather than against reason, is the necessary precondition for
any universal human vision, but this in itself does not translate into the language of prayer and worship that constitutes
a personal relationship with God. The God of the
Enlightenment philosophers was a creator God who retained
the attributes of omniscience, omnipotence, transcendence
and implicit masculinity with which Christian theologians
had endowed him, but he was no longer the God incarnate in
Christ who was intimately involved with and attentive to our
human condition and accessible to consciousness.

For Christian feminists, there is a need to incarnate
Christ anew in the western understanding of God, through
a prayerful and informed engagement with what the

Christian tradition has said about God made human in Christ. This means respecting the integrity of the Christian narrative, and resisting the pressure to conform to an agenda set by the dictates of secularism or driven by social and ethical concerns that are not rooted in the Christian understanding of the relationship between God and humankind. Christians can and must work with people of all faiths and none for the transformation of the world, but this does not entail a loss or denial of Christian identity. Indeed, identity and difference are the precondition for fruitful dialogue and exchange in all our relationships and encounters. To realize this means recognizing the ways in which the symbols and stories of the Christian faith require us always to be open to the other, to acknowledge the limitations of our own knowledge and understanding, and to see the revelation of God at work in all creation, including all peoples with their many cultures, religions and histories. It also means recognizing that the vitality and dynamism of the Christian faith cannot be reduced to a set of moral values or a rational proposition about the world, because a living and vibrant faith is communicated primarily by means of symbols, sacraments and practices that derive their potency from their capacity to stimulate and energize creative, imaginative performances of hope.

So if postmodern woman is to find herself anew in God, the solution lies neither in an appeal to premodern Christianity nor in an appeal to the God of the philosophers. Resisting the seductions of a naive nostalgia for faith without reason on the one hand, and the hubristic claims of reason without faith on the other, the task for women is to listen to a multitude of voices, past and present, to ask anew what kind of relationship there is between female humanity and God. This is a task that is only just beginning as we enter the third millennium, and its implications for the Christian faith are vast because it requires a radical transformation in the methods, language and values of theology. It is not simply a case of 'add woman and stir', but of finding a whole new way of speaking about God, humankind and nature from the perspective of the other side of humanity made in the image of God – the side that has until now been a silent and shadowy figure in the story of salvation.

For some, this entails making women's experience the starting point for theological reflection, as a corrective to the unacknowledged influence that men's experience has had on Christian theology so far. According to Rosemary Radford Ruether:

> The critical principle of feminist theology is the promotion of the full humanity of women. Whatever denies, diminishes, or distorts the full humanity of women is, therefore, appraised as not redemptive. Theologically speaking, whatever diminishes or denies the full humanity of women must be presumed not to reflect the divine or an authentic relation to the divine, or to reflect the authentic nature of things, or to be the message or work of an authentic redeemer or a community of redemption.
>
> This negative principle also implies the positive principle: what does promote the full humanity of women is of the Holy, it does reflect true relation to the divine, it is the true nature of things, the authentic message of redemption and the mission of redemptive community.[2]

Ruether's approach has had a formative influence on the development of feminist theology, but I remain uneasy about this privileging of the full humanity of woman as the basis for theology. The question of what is meant by 'full humanity' seems to me to be the great mystery of our existence, and indeed this book begins and ends with that question. What does it mean for a woman to be fully human? Ultimately, the Christian tradition teaches that the fullness of our humanity is hidden in God, and only in union with God for all eternity will we discover what that means. Women's experience, although it has a vital role to play, cannot in and of itself be a reliable starting point for theological reflection, nor can it tell us what it means to be fully human. Rather, we must think about the question of God and of our own existence in that mysterious space of encounter between the body and language, and between our personal stories and the larger cultural and religious narratives that shape our lives. The image of the 'thinking heart' is sometimes used by eastern Christian writers to describe the task of theology. The thinking heart is also the praying heart, and it is from this starting point of prayer, reflection and feeling, situated between the human condition and the divine vocation, that theology 'happens'.

But of course, prayer itself is an experience. It is a way of consciously experiencing ourselves as creatures who come before the mystery of God as we are, seeking wisdom, consolation or transformation from where we find ourselves in the human story. So the most contemplative or prayerful theology remains deeply rooted in the soil of human experience, even as it is brought to life and sustained by the warmth and light of divine revelation. This means that even the most inspired theology is always invested with the cultural, historical and psychological narratives of our particular ways of being human. Theology is not the pure science of God – there could be no such thing, because we can only ever speak of God from within historical and linguistic frameworks that provide us with a distinctive set of images and ideas that we associate with the divine. Revelation is filtered through all our human perceptions and experiences, and it cannot be separated from these in a way that would give us access to the distilled truth of God.

However, feminist theology makes visible what has been largely hidden and unacknowledged in the theological tradition, because it situates theology in its cultural contexts and seeks to identify the various preconceived beliefs about gender, society and God that have influenced the ways in which Christians have read the scriptures and formulated doctrine. Like all theology, feminist theology, too, is culturally conditioned, informed as it is by the questions women ask of the Church today. The difference is, traditional theology has tended to present itself as an objective way of knowing and speaking about God, whereas feminist theology, in common with postmodernist theories of knowledge, points to the impossibility of such objective knowledge and, in acknowledging the subjectivity of all ways of knowing, seeks to make theological discourse more truthful by challenging its claims to be The Truth.

To say this is not to deny the content of revelation, the divine inspiration of the scriptures, nor the objective existence of God. For some theologians, these all ultimately become factors of language and culture: our ways of speaking about God are just that – ways of speaking that have no external reference points in reality. I resist this dissolution of the substance of faith into language alone, because it is perfectly reasonable to acknowledge that all we know of God we know in human terms, in language, images and ideas that bear the content of our humanity rather than the essence of the divinity, while believing that, nevertheless, there is an objective reality that approximates our ways of speaking about God. In subscribing to the Christian faith, I believe that God is the self-revealing Trinity, that the second person of that Trinity became incarnate and lived as part of our history in a way that allows for a perfect union between God's life and ours through the redemption of the cosmos, and that the scriptures, although humanly authored and culturally conditioned, are nevertheless stained-glass windows through which the light of God obliquely shines.

This means approaching the theological tradition of the Christian faith with a sense of expectation and attentiveness with regard to the light of revelation, even while recognizing that this tradition is distorted by the perceptions of men who have formed an exclusive community of interpretation. In part, this task means healing the division that opened up between the language of theology and the language of spirituality and prayer in the twelfth century, when the universities began to take over from the abbeys and monasteries as the locus of theological reflection. Before then, although women did not occupy positions of authority within the Church, they were at least able to contribute to the formulation of theology in mixed communities where men and women could exchange ideas and had access to the same language and symbols. This educated group was of course a very small and privileged minority, but it meant the active participation of women in the production of theology. An early example of this is Gregory of Nyssa's work, *On the Soul and Resurrection*, which was primarily inspired by the reflections of his sister Macrina, whom he refers to as 'the Teacher'. But with the rise of the universities in the twelfth and thirteenth centuries, theological education became the exclusive prerogative of ordained and celibate men, who began to develop ever more complicated and abstract structures of logic and argumentation that eventually came to be known as Scholasticism. Women were discouraged from learning Latin, which was the official language of the schools and which is still the language in which Catholic doctrine is formulated. Instead, women expressed themselves in the vernacular, which resulted in a growing rift between the languages of theology and spirituality at the level of both meaning and syntax. The language of theology became increasingly rationalized, structured and intellectual, while the language of devotion and spirituality became the language of affectivity, spontaneity and the human experience of God, often expressed through women's voices, or through the feminized voice of the male soul speaking as the bride and lover of Christ. Thus it is perhaps not far-fetched to suggest that, if women do indeed have 'a different voice' as Gilligan argues, that voice became particularly marked by sexual difference from the time of the twelfth century. Today, a postmodern climate of enquiry and openness to new methods and approaches to knowledge are allowing for the reintegration of these various perspectives, so that theology is once again able to express itself in fluid and poetic forms of language that can accommodate both the rationality and the affectivity of belief.

The task for feminist theologians then is not to discard the theological tradition but to break it open to voices of difference. The story of a woman anointing Jesus occurs in different forms in all four Gospels. According to Mark's Gospel:

Jesus was at Bethany in the house of Simon the leper; he was at dinner when a woman came in with an alabaster jar of very costly ointment, pure nard. She broke the jar and poured the ointment on his head. Some who were there said to one another indignantly, 'Why this waste of ointment? Ointment like this could have been sold for over three hundred denarii and the money given to the poor'; and they were angry with her. But Jesus said, 'Leave her alone. Why are you upsetting her? What she has done for me is one of the good works. You have the poor with you always, and you can be kind to them whenever you wish, but you will not always have me. She has done what was in her

power to do: she has anointed my body beforehand for
its burial. I tell you solemnly, wherever throughout all
the world the Good News is proclaimed, what she has
done will be told also, in remembrance of her' (Mark
14:3–9).

Today, women must expect to be scolded by those who
have appointed themselves as sole custodians of the Word
of God, as we break open the jar of men's carefully con-
tained theology to release anew the fragrance of God's
presence among us. We can perform this as an anointing,
as an act of prayerful remembrance and hope for the ways
in which women have always recognized the body of Christ
among us. This means considering what theology has said
about women and God, recognizing the ways in which the
light of revelation has been obscured by social and psychological factors arising out of the conditions in which theology has been produced, but still expecting to find glimmers
of truthfulness that provide a reason for women to remain
within this story of faith and decipher anew its meanings
and promises.

From this perspective, theological reflection entails
study and prayer, mourning and celebration, but it also
entails the awareness that for women no less than for men,
theology as an intellectual discipline is fraught with the
risk of hubris. Rowan Williams suggests that, 'Talking
theologically, talking of how religion avoids becoming the
most dramatically empty and power-obsessed discourse
imaginable, is necessary and very difficult.'[3] There are
feminist theologians whose rhetorical style takes the form
of moralizing and preaching, sometimes informed by a profound hostility towards all things male and masculine, and
grounded in the absolute conviction that God is on their
side. Such theology serves as a reminder that the word
'God' is always and perhaps inextricably enmeshed in the

discourses of power and domination, even when it is used from the positions of those who regard themselves as in some sense marginal or powerless vis-à-vis the dominant tradition.

So even as feminists seek to introduce into Christian theology the language and images of woman's becoming, we must recognize that 'God' functions in several ways in theological discourse. It is a word that is used to disguise the structures of power and domination that so often inform the theological agenda, whether that is traditional 'malestream' theology or more recent liberationist and feminist theologies. But the word 'God' also points to the absolute otherness and mystery of God, in relation to whom theology can only ever be the language of invocation, prayer and yearning, shaped and nurtured in the matrix of the believing community. To quote Williams again:

> God is there not to supply what is lacking in mortal knowledge or mortal power, but simply as the source, sustainer and end of our mortality. The hope professed by Christians of immortal life cannot be a hope for a non-mortal way of seeing the world; it is rather trust that what our mortality teaches us of God opens up the possibility of knowing God or seeing God in ways for which we have, by definition, no useful mortal words.[4]

For Williams, the community of prayer safeguards the integrity and honesty of theology. It keeps religious language open to its own limitations and incompleteness before God, making it live with 'the constant possibility of its own relativizing, interruption, silencing; it will not regard its conclusions as having authority independently of their relation to the critical, penitent community it seeks to help to be itself'.[5]

But if silence stands guard over the hubris of theological language, it is nevertheless important to find ways of talking about God that open into a prayerful playground of the spirit. In Proverbs 8, God's wisdom describes herself as being 'ever at play in God's presence, at play everywhere in God's world' (Prov. 8:30). The image of play can serve as an antidote to power. It suggests an environment of trust as well as of learning, but it is also a reminder not to take ourselves too seriously by investing our theological speculations with claims to divine authority. Our language about God is of necessity a language about ourselves – the worlds we inhabit or invent, the terrors we encounter or imagine, the hopes we cherish or fulfil. In this context, God becomes both the imaginary companion of our conversations, like the imaginary friends of childhood who often seemed vividly real and present, and the inaccessible Other whom Catherine of Siena calls 'the fire and abyss of love'. Playful theology, aware of its own limitations, does not seek to describe or to define God but rather to discover a space of creative expression, a space of laughter and tears, within the fire and abyss of God's love.

Donald Nicholl, in a moving reflection on the vocation of theology, writes of 'the vein of sadness and tragedy which runs through all our efforts to know'.[6] He refers to Aquinas's suggestion that the beatitude of mourning is 'the special beatitude for those whose calling it is to extend the boundaries of knowledge. . . . [W]henever our minds yearn towards some new truth, then we become afflicted with pain, because our whole being wishes to protect the balance of inertia and comfort which we have established for ourselves'.[7]

Reflecting on this idea of theology as mourning, I found myself wondering if perhaps Eve might be the patron saint of feminist theology, for she symbolizes the loss of innocence and the experience of alienation that necessarily accompanies the acquisition of knowledge. The influential Old Testament scholar Phyllis Trible argues that in the story of Genesis, it is Eve who converses theologically with the serpent, weighing up her options and taking responsibility for her actions. The woman is, says Trible, 'both theologian and translator'.[8]

Like Eve, the theologian must leave the paradise of unquestioning intimacy and union with God, in order to pursue the question of God through the alienating wilderness of culture and learning. So often, in my own prayer and reflections and in the experiences of women I teach, I realize the gulf that opens up when one allows feminist consciousness to inform one's relationship to God, to the Church and to the Christian tradition. When I look back at my diaries and jottings of twenty years ago, I see an unproblematic quest for a Father God, played out in the language and symbols of a faith defined by masculine pronouns, structures and values. I have had to ask myself what it means to introduce a devout Christian woman to the questions that feminism asks of the Church, when I know that I risk disordering the world of innocence that she has always inhabited. And yet I also know that, time and again, I have worked with women whose faith has moved into that strange space of encounter between feminist consciousness and the Christian tradition, and among those women I have had some of my richest experiences of a living theology informed by study, prayer and an active commitment to those on the margins of society. So the woman who responds to the challenge of feminism while remaining faithful to her Christian faith might find symbolic resonances between her own dilemma and that of Eve. She is offered a strange form of knowledge, and she must weigh up the options that confront her. Should she simply say 'no', remain obedient to the rules and laws that she has been taught, and forego forever that desire to know and understand more than is good for her? In the Jewish tradition, the decision to eat the fruit is not always portrayed as an act of wilful defiance against God. It is sometimes portrayed as the originating moment in human moral freedom, when our primal forebears broke free of the tyranny of the gods, to take responsibility for the world and their place within it.[9]

But Eve also stands as a caution to us in our quest for unlimited knowledge. Like her, the theologian must recognize that the desire for knowledge is opaque and vulnerable to hubris – the temptation to use knowledge to acquire the power of gods. That is why the relationship between Eve and Mary, defined not in terms of the ancient oppositions of masculine theology, but as a complex interweaving of themes of sin and redemption, is rich symbolic terrain for feminist thought. Eve symbolizes the bargain with the death that knowledge entails – the death of innocence and the death of certainty that so often follow upon the acquisition of knowledge. But Mary symbolizes the faithfulness and the promise of life that true knowledge of God offers, for such knowledge is always open to divine grace. Mary is the 'New Eve', in whom Eve's dilemma is resolved and transformed through the liberating acceptance of Christ as the one who comes bodily into our human predicament and reconciles the irreconcilable oppositions, born of the knowledge of good and evil, that tear us apart. Only in prayer, communal Christian endeavour and faithfulness does theology escape its implication in the sin that ensnared Eve, and taste the liberation of human knowing in Mary's conception of Christ.

This also means recognizing that Eve is the 'mother of the living'. In Mary, Eve is renewed and is at last enabled to turn her knowledge to the service of life rather than death. Her theology offers not condemnation but new life and hope to the children of God, being ever attentive to the weak and the hungry, to the newborn visions that seed themselves in the human spirit and cry out for the knowledge of God. No theologian can provide that knowledge, but he or she can attentively, tenderly, listen and respond with a language that might help to give substance and nurture to the yearning of the spirit.

The Christian story draws us into a space of paradox and mystery beyond the dualistic knowledge of good and evil that is Eve's bequest to us. This is the basis for its vision of salvation with all its social, sexual and moral ramifications. Word becomes flesh, the divine becomes human, and the finite, material world is drawn into the eternal life of God through the power of forgiving and reconciling love. This story has a mythical beginning in paradise and a promised ending in heaven. Its history unfolds around the pivotal moment of the incarnation, and its material reality is played out in the life of the community of faith that is the Church. It is a tragi-comedy, as full of pathos and failure as it is of transformation and joy. In the National Gallery's touring exhibition on the theme of 'Paradise', the publicity material included the saying that 'Paradox ends where paradise begins.' The life of faith calls us to accept the paradox of living in a space of continual flux between this world and the next, between the body and God, between society and the kingdom of God, between the knowledge of good and evil and the reconciliation of all things in Christ, and to recognize and celebrate those fleeting epiphanies of paradise that break through the paradox as a foretaste of the world to come.

---

[1] John Ruskin, 'Of Queens' Gardens' in *Sesame and Lilies* (London: Thomas Nelson & Sons, 1865), p. 82.

[2] Rosemary Radford Ruether, *Sexism and God-Talk – Towards a Feminist Theology* (London: SCM, 1992), pp. 18–19.

[3] Rowan Williams, 'Theological Integrity' in *On Christian Theology* (Oxford: Blackwell Publishers, 2000), p. 15.

[4] Ibid., p. 14.

[5] Ibid., p. 13.

[6] Donald Nicholl, *The Beatitude of Truth: Reflections of a Lifetime* (London: Darton, Longman & Todd, 1997), p. 5.

7   Ibid., pp. 5–6.
8   Phyllis Trible, 'Eve and Adam: Genesis 2–3 Reread' in Carol P. Christ and Judith Plaskow (eds.), *Womanspirit Rising: A Feminist Reader in Religion* (San Francisco: HarperSanFrancisco, 1979), p. 79.
9   See Jonathan Magonet, *A Rabbi's Bible* (London: SCM Press, 1991); Tikva Frymer-Kensky, *In the Wake of the Goddesses: Women, Culture and the Biblical Transformation of Pagan Myth* (New York: Fawcett Columbine, 1992), p. 109.

4
Women, Language and God

When women's experience is expressed in a church whose tradition is machistic, the other side of human experience returns to theological discourse: the side of the person who gives birth, nurses, nourishes, of the person who for centuries has remained silent with regard to anything having to do with theology. Now she begins to express her experience of God, in another manner, a manner that does not demand that reason alone be regarded as the single and universal mediation of theological discourse. This way of doing theology includes what is vital, utilizing mediations that can help to express what has been experienced, without exhausting it, a discourse that leads to the awareness that there is always something more, something that words cannot express.

Ivone Gebara[1]

If we accept that Christian theological reflection takes place in a space of paradox and mystery, so that it moves restlessly between words and silence, between history and eternity, between immanence and transcendence, then we must also recognize the theological vocation to dwell in the *aporia* between language and the body as the true locus of Christian reflection on the nature of God. The body is central to the Christian faith, because the doctrine of the incarnation encompasses the material world, including the human body. That was Christianity's great scandal to the philosophers and believers of the ancient world. They could accept a religion that promised spiritual perfection

beyond the body's corruption and finitude. They could
believe in a God who briefly appeared in human form –
such epiphanies were common among the Greek and
Roman gods. But they could not accept a faith that identified God so completely with the human body that it dared
to claim that Jesus was fully human and fully divine, that
in him God was born and died like any other mortal being,
and that when he rose on the third day the whole material
world began its rising to eternal life through him and with
him. If the early Church had been willing to say that Jesus
was fully human and had something of the divine about
him, or if it had been willing to say that Jesus was fully
divine and only appeared to be human, either of those
claims would have gained converts among the intellectuals
of the time. But to suggest that the perfection of God could
become a body born of a woman and crucified on the cross
without being defiled and corrupted, militated against
everything that philosophers believed could rationally and
morally be said about God.

Protestant Christianity has traditionally been wary of
what it means to say that in Christ the whole physical
world is sanctified. Particularly in Calvinist forms of
Protestantism, the belief that the fall resulted in the total
corruption of the material world deprives nature of any
intrinsic grace, so that Christ becomes the exclusive source
of revelation and grace, and the natural world is reduced to
a state of meaningless passivity outside of that revelation.
The great twentieth-century Protestant theologian Karl
Barth vigorously rejected the idea that there can be a natural theology, developed not only in conversation with
scripture but also through the appreciation of nature. But
Catholicism has always insisted that natural grace was corrupted but not destroyed in the fall. All human beings
retain a capacity – however distorted and partial – to sense
the presence of God through the residual activity of grace

in creation. The graced work of creation continues, and every rational being is able to recognize something of the truth, wonder and goodness of God through nature. This means that the human body too has revelatory potential, including its sexual characteristics.

The feminist reconstruction of theology therefore involves negotiating the inscrutable terrain that constitutes the gap between language and the body, in a way that allows the female body to occupy that sacramental space for the first time as a person made in the image of God, fully equal to and different from the male body. This is the task of symbolic reclamation that is the precondition of every social and ethical vision that might arise out of a new appreciation of the relationship between God and creation, seen through the eyes of women. And this means interrogating first and foremost the significance of the body, since it is the body that is invested with the sexual meanings that position us as gendered beings in the social and domestic constructs that constitute the world of human relationships.

To construct a theology of woman out of the vast libraries of Christian texts, one has to unpick the tapestry of meanings that has been woven like a straightjacket around the female body, in order to stand naked with Eve before God and ask anew, Who am I? Who are you? But of course, such original nakedness is impossible. Our naked bodies are as inscrutable to us as the face of God, for we see and understand them only through the meanings that have been mapped onto them by language and culture, including theology. In his reflection on the Book of Genesis, *Original Unity of Man and Woman*, John Paul II describes the original nakedness of the man and woman in the Garden of Eden as signifying the capacity of the sexes to come to a full awareness of embodiment as male and female through one another. The words 'they were not ashamed' (Gen. 2:25) 'do not express a lack, but, on the contrary, serve to indicate a particular fullness of consciousness and experience, above all a fullness of understanding of the meaning of the body, bound up with the fact that "they were naked"'.[2] The fall brings about a corruption of the knowledge that allowed man and woman to discover the meaning of the body in nakedness and freedom. Now, the human being seeks knowledge through 'the veil of shame'[3] that complicates the nuptial meaning of the body, and 'the horizon of death extends over the whole perspective of human life on earth'.[4]

For women, the veil of shame that prevents us from understanding the meaning of our bodies is partly woven out of the language of sin and denigration that men have used to hide the original glory of Eve. When Tertullian in the second century included all women in his condemnation of Eve, he became one of the first Christian thinkers in a tradition of contempt that has spanned two millennia. Writing on female dress, Tertullian exhorts women to 'go about in humble garb, and rather to affect meanness of appearance, walking about as Eve mourning and repentant, in order that by every garb of penitence she might the more fully expiate that which she derives from Eve, – the ignominy, I mean, of the first sin, and the odium (attaching to her as the cause) of human perdition'. He continues:

And do you not know that you are (each) an Eve? The sentence of God on this sex of yours lives in this age: the guilt must of necessity live too. *You* are the devil's gateway: *you* are the unsealer of that (forbidden) tree: *you* are the first deserter of the divine law: *you* are she who persuaded him whom the devil was not valiant enough to attack. *You* destroyed so easily God's image, man. On account of *your* desert – that is, death – even the Son of God had to die.[5]

Thus, from the beginning, Christianity has failed to fully acknowledge women as forgiven and redeemed members of the body of Christ. While women have indeed been included in the promise of salvation, the lingering belief that the female body remains culpable because of Eve's sin, and must therefore continue to bear the punishment and consequences of that sin, has not only contradicted the doctrine that Christ's suffering brings forgiveness and salvation to the world, it has also been played out in a long history of the persecution, abuse and negation of women's personhood and dignity in the Christian social order.

How can a woman escape such a Babel of condemnation, to discover herself anew as a creature made in the image of God and restored to her original goodness through baptism in Christ? The answer lies not in a futile quest for a new language, because we cannot invent language. We are born into it, inherit it, inhabit it and pass it on, but we do not create it. However, as dictators and ideologues know, we can change its meanings. There is a famous exchange in Lewis Carroll's *Through the Looking Glass*, which points to the close relationship between mastery and meaning:

'When *I* use a word,' Humpty Dumpty said, in a rather scornful tone, 'it means just what I choose it to mean – neither more nor less.'

'The question is,' said Alice, 'whether you *can* make words mean different things.'

'The question is,' said Humpty Dumpty, 'which is to be master – that's all.'[6]

If, as a feminist theologian, I accept that the core symbols of Christian theology – the Trinity, the incarnation, death and resurrection of Jesus Christ, the revelation of Scripture and the communion of the Church – are true, but also that their truth is veiled by the language and ideology of masculinity, then the task is not to strip away the veil of language but to try to look through different veils, to unleash new symbolic meanings. This means avoiding the mastery of language that comes from a kind of censorial *diktat* – and much political correctness is guilty of such linguistic dictatorship – and seeking instead the liberation of language through exploring the many possibilities that open up when we appreciate the fluidity and indeed the volatility of symbolic meanings.

We can never 'see' God, which is to say that we can never have an understanding of God that is not clouded by our own muddled perceptions and preconceptions. Whatever we mean by fallenness, the Christian reading of Genesis, like the Freudian Oedipus complex, acknowledges the extent to which there is a primal sense of alienation and loss at the heart of the human condition. We are estranged from God, from one another and from nature, and we experience ourselves as fragile creatures who must struggle for survival in a wilderness of work and pain. That wilderness is nothing more nor less than culture itself. It is our creative endeavour to express meaning, truth and hope, played out in the language and artefacts of human existence by which we seek to defy death's annihilating silence. We experience this as a wilderness of struggle because, unlike Adam and Eve in the Garden of Eden, we do not live in a world of transparent meanings and truths. We do not name the world as Adam did, because it has already been named. We do not gaze at one another, male and female, with eyes of wonder and joy, because our vision is clouded by blame, by twisted desire, and by the abuse of power. We do not walk with God in the garden, because God has disappeared and left us with only a word – 'God' – that bears an echo, a memory, a haunting of the spirit. So nature, sexuality and God have become part of the wilderness experience, a wilderness in which language and culture must represent but can never recreate the world we long for as our memory and hope of paradise.

As women we cannot stand naked beside Eve in the presence of God, for our existence is already clothed in language and our bodies are already mapped by meanings. Without these maps, we do not know who we are, but we are coming to recognize that the maps we have are not accurate. Perhaps an analogy would be the introduction of the Peters Projection World Map by historian and cartographer Dr Arno Peters in 1974. This map takes into account the contours of the globe in reproducing the sizes of the land masses and continents. This means that the northern hemisphere takes up a smaller proportion of the whole, and the African continent seems much larger than on the old Mercator Projection Map, first designed in the sixteenth century and reflecting the perceptions of a world dominated by Europe. Theologically, women today face a similar task. We must draw new maps that give us a clearer sense of perspective about God, nature and humankind, by bringing the female body into sharper relief as a person made in the image and likeness of God. The metaphor of mapping is appropriate for this activity because, as Paula Cooey points out, 'Mapping is visual and spatial, as well as temporal and verbal. It further preserves a tension between materiality and discourse that I find lacking in such concepts as "interpreting" and "expressing," though "mapping" includes connotations of both.'[7] The question is, given that we must work with the resources we already have if we seek to remain a coherent and integral part of the Christian story, how can women find 'a different voice' within that story, expressing a different bodily relationship to God?

The dominant language of theology obscures rather than reveals the meaning of God in woman and woman in God, but Christian theology comes in many forms, and the systematic arguments and doctrinal debates that have

preoccupied men through the centuries represent only one
way of doing theology. Every believer is a theologian of
everyday life, in so far as she or he incorporates the doctrines and values of a religious tradition into a living and
embodied faith. In this sense, there have been many women
theologians. A few have been remembered because their
ideas were approved of and preserved by a male hierarchy,
such as Catherine of Siena and Teresa of Avila. Others are
accessible to us today because their writings lay undiscov-
ered and forgotten for centuries, such as Hildegard of
Bingen. But there are many thousands who have been
forgotten because they were deemed too insignificant or too
heretical for their ideas to be preserved, and we can only
guess what a theology of woman might be like if we knew
the silenced visions and dreams of all those who were
burned at the stake, cloistered behind high walls, or denied
access to an education that would have allowed them to
record their ideas for future generations.

Yet today as never before, we can begin to gather together
the voices and visions of women, to imaginatively fill in the
gaps, and to redraw the maps of the Christian faith in a
way that faithfully represents the contours and boundaries
of female existence. Pope John Paul II refers to masculinity
and femininity as being based on 'two different "incarna-
tions," that is, on two ways of "being a body"'.[8] He says,
'The body, in fact, and it alone, is capable of making visible
what is invisible: the spiritual and the divine. . . . [I]n his
body as male or female, man feels he is a subject of holiness.'[9] But if this is the case, then there are also two ways
of doing theology, two ways of reflecting on what it means
to be made in the image and likeness of God, and so far
Christianity has only developed its thinking with regard to
one of these ways. It is not possible for communities of
men, however learned and well-intentioned, to produce
authentic knowledge of women's relationships to God, to

men and to one another. All they will produce are ideological constructs that blur the truth and diminish rather
than enrich the Christian story. The tradition thus needs
to be dismantled in its teachings on women, and the story
of creation, incarnation, salvation and resurrection must
be broken open to allow new possibilities to emerge, as
women reflect systematically but also poetically on the
meaning of this story for them.

However, the relationship between the body and theology
is, as I suggested above, complicated by a number of factors.
On the one hand, any theology of sexual difference must
accord the body a place of significance in the construction
of language. Whatever subtle psychological and spiritual
differences may or may not exist between men and women,
and whether or not these can be attributed to nature, to
nurture, or to a bit of both, the most obvious and immediate marker of sexual difference is the body itself. In
acknowledging that we understand the meaning of our
bodies only through language, I think it is important not to
adopt the extreme dualism of modern critical theorists
such as Jacques Derrida, who would deny any intrinsic,
pre-linguistic significance to the body. Every human being
who has made love, held a child, laughed or cried with
another, experienced the body's tenderness or violence,
knows that our bodies are capable of wordless eloquence in
gesture, touch and gaze. But such meanings depend on the
present, on the immediacy of our material selves to one
another in time and space. As soon as the bodily moment
passes, it must be recalled and recreated in language, and
from then on the experience is one of recollection and
reflection, not immediate perception.

That is why I am wary of certain forms of romantic
feminism that exalt the female body with its sexual and
maternal capacities as the material locus of feminist
thought. Instead of seeking equality with men on grounds

of rationality and justice, this kind of feminism seeks to establish the female body as a repository of ancient knowledge and insight. Because a woman menstruates, gestates, gives birth, feeds and nurtures the young, because her life is marked by transitions through stages of fertility, from childhood to the menarche to the menopause, this is seen to give her access to greater intuitive knowledge and greater empathy with nature. While masculine rationality, with its fear of the body and its privileging of the abstract, the spiritual and the transcendent, sees female embodiment as a site of terror and chaos, for romantic feminists it is a sacred site of empowerment, fecundity and sexual wisdom. In its celebration of motherhood – although not in its desire to unleash the power of female sexuality! – this form of feminism has much in common with some aspects of conservative Catholicism, not least with the theology of John Paul II.

However, this celebration of the body too often masks the fact that it is talking not about bodies *per se* but about alternative linguistic constructs, where the metaphors and symbols associated with abstract masculinity are replaced by the metaphors and symbols of female embodiment. This is particularly important if one bears in mind that those advocating this linguistic transformation are usually women academics working in an environment that by its very nature makes them theoreticians of the body. I say this as a woman academic who also spent many years of my adult life in the home caring for four young children, before I became a mature student and began a new career. There was a physical immediacy to those maternal years – a tangible daily involvement in the body, a constant aura of blood, milk and excrement, a rich pattern of menstruation, sexuality, pregnancy, childbirth and lactation that marked out the rhythms of my life. But I no longer live like that, and I certainly have no wish to return to that way of living until perhaps old age or illness force it upon me in different and challenging forms. I am glad of this transition to a way of living and working that allows me the time and space, and also the education, to reflect upon and theorize about those experiences through bringing them into conversation with an intellectual tradition. If those years had a physical intimacy that I often miss, they were also often marked by a deep sense of intellectual frustration that I do not miss at all.

To recognize the disjunction between our bodily experiences, the concepts we use to understand these, and the language we use to interpret them, it is necessary to acknowledge that dualism has constructive as well as destructive potential. Dualistic thinking is seen as unequivocally negative by many feminists, implying as it does a false sense of separation between matter and the spirit. But some form of dualism is inescapable if we are to transcend the intimacies and particularities of everyday life to interpret our experiences in more universal terms. I am fortunate that I have come into the academic world at a time when feminism has made it possible to theorize about the body in ways that can accommodate the language of sexuality, motherhood and of women's experience, so that the task of intellectual reflection is one not of denial but of rearranging one's priorities, of negotiating the sometimes conflicting demands of living fully in the body and creating spaces for the mind. To say this is not to posit a dualistic distinction between mind and body that actually exists, but to acknowledge that these are valuable metaphors that express what it feels like to experience the difference between sensation and reflection, between a bodily experience and an intellectual process. For women who are mothers, it is also I believe an honest recognition of the ways in which we find ourselves constantly juggling the demands of professional worlds that rarely accommodate

the physical and emotional realities of the relationship
between mothers and children, and the legitimate desire to
be part of those worlds and to have lives beyond the domestic sphere. Mary Gordon, in her novel *Men and Angels*,
expresses what this struggle between motherhood and
work entails for the central character, Anne Foster:

> And there was the other part of mother love: it was not
> all of life. And that was wonderful; it was a tremendous
> mercy. . . You could turn, sometimes, from the sight of
> them, making their way in the world, so dangerous, so
> treacherous; you could put down the burden of that
> mother love, could swim up from it, passing the exhil-
> arating sights, the colourful quick fish, the shining
> rocks and bubbles. And pass, too, the clumps of weeds.
> There was all that in the world that was apart from
> them: intractable, too, and difficult, eluding what you
> wanted to say of it, impossible to compass or get right.
> . . . And then, refreshed, she could dive back down to
> the dense underworld, to her children, and say, 'This is
> life. What shall we make of it?'[10]

This is quite different from the violent and destructive
dualism that has prevailed in the western intellectual
tradition, and that is still the dominant language of much
western theology and philosophy. Such thinking denies the
significance of the body, and still refuses to acknowledge the
ways in which sexuality and embodiment shape language as
pervasively through their absence as through their symbolic presence. For as feminists have shown time and again
through their analyses of men's philosophical and theological writings, the body *in absentia* is the male body, and its
presence leaks through the cracks and gaps in meaning
with a corrosive influence on coherence and truth.

But for feminist scholars, there is risk as well as opportunity in identifying women with the language of the body, because that might simply reinforce existing stereotypes. Men have always associated femininity with the body and masculinity with the mind, and in affirming the significance of the body for language and thought, it is important for women scholars not to sacrifice the demands of rationality and coherence to a kind of woolly-minded romanticism. For women as well as for men, the body is not unambiguous in its demands, functions and desires. We too are prey to appetites and impulses that militate against our capacity for wholeness, and we too need to construct ethical and linguistic values that recognize both the body's potential and its limitations. Even as we find ways to celebrate the female body's capacity for self-expression, joy and communion through sensuality, sexuality, sacramentality and maternity, we also need to be mindful that our bodies have a capacity to wound, to betray, to neglect and to destroy. Thus feminist theological language needs to develop its own insights into the particular ways in which female bodies experience sin and grace as the formative dimensions of the Christian life played out between the mystery of our origins and endings.

To understand the symbolic significance of this, one must see the incarnation as the telescopic vantage point from which Christians look back to the beginning and forward to the ending of the human story. The Christian doxology, 'as it was in the beginning is now and ever shall be, world without end, Amen', has particular resonance with regard to the story of creation and redemption. As God made the world in the beginning, when it was very good and free from sin and death, so the world is now in Christ, and so the world will be forever in heaven. This means that interpretations of the Book of Genesis have profound implications for the Christian understanding of the relationship between God and creation, between humankind and nature, and between male and female, in the beginning, now and for all eternity. As has already been apparent in this chapter, Christian thinking about the meaning of the sexed female body consistently refers to the figure of Eve as a prototype that determines the place of woman in creation as willed by God. With this in mind, I turn now to consider more closely the ways in which theological ideas about human sexuality have been influenced by readings of Genesis.

1   Ivone Gebara, 'Women Doing Theology in Latin America' in Elsa Tamez (ed.), *Through Her Eyes: Women's Theology from Latin America* (Maryknoll, NY: Orbis Books, 1989), pp. 39–41.

2   John Paul II, *Original Unity of Man and Woman – Catechesis on the Book of Genesis* (Boston, MA: St. Paul Books & Media, 1981), p. 94.

3   Ibid., p. 143.

4   Ibid., p. 165.

5   Tertullian, 'On the Apparel of Women', trans. Rev. S. Thelwall, in *The Ante-Nicene Fathers*, vol. IV (Edinburgh: T & T Clark; Grand Rapids, MI: William B. Eerdmans Publishing Co., repr. 1994), pp. 3–6.

6   Lewis Carroll, *Through the Looking Glass* (London: J.M. Dent & Sons, 1979), p. 79.

7   Paula M. Cooey, *Religious Imagination and the Body: A Feminist Analysis* (New York and Oxford: Oxford University Press, 1994), p. 91

8   John Paul II, *Original Unity*, p. 62.

9   Ibid., p. 144–5.

10 Mary Gordon, *Men and Angels* (Harmondsworth: Penguin Books, 1986), pp. 319–20.

5
Woman, Man and Creation

Because Tom is a man, because I love him dearly, I
haven't told him what I believe: that the world is split
in two, between those who are handed power at birth,
at gestation, encoded with a seemingly random chro-
mosome determinate that says yes for ever and ever,
and those like Norah, like Danielle Westerman, like
my mother, like my mother-in-law, like me, like all of
us who fall into the uncoded female otherness in
which the power to assert ourselves and claim our
lives has been displaced by a compulsion to shut down
our bodies and seal our mouths and be as nothing
against the fireworks and streaking stars and blinding
light of the Big Bang. That's the problem.

This cry is overstated; I'm an editor, after all, and
recognize purple ink when I see it. The sentiment is
excessive, blowsy, loose, womanish. But I am willing to
blurt it all out, if only to myself. Blurting is a form of
bravery. I'm just catching on to that fact. Arriving
late, as always.

Carol Shields, *Unless*[1]

The story of creation and the fall in Genesis had no great
significance for pre-Christian Jewish thinkers. There is
only a passing reference to it in the other books of the Old
Testament, and it does not feature prominently among
other ancient Jewish writings. However, the early Church
saw the incarnation as a new creation, with the Pauline
letters several times referring to Christ as the New Adam.
By the middle of the second century, Justin and Irenaeus

were writing about Mary as the New Eve, so that the myth
of Genesis was from the beginning embedded within the
symbols and metaphors of the Christian faith, in a poetic
theological vision that resisted systematization through its
fluidity of language and symbolism. The mystery of the
incarnation could not be explained or defined. It could only
be alluded to in language that invited the spirit into a place
of mystical contemplation and wonder, moving restlessly
from image to image as it sought to draw the human imagination into the impossible meeting space of Word/flesh,
God/human, spirit/body. In this emerging symbolic world,
Mary was compared to the virgin earth of paradise from
which the second Adam was created, and to Eve as the first
woman of the new creation.

But although the church fathers were elaborating a
theology of salvation rather than condemnation for women
as well as for men – Eve and all women were redeemed in
Mary – they were also setting in place a language of sexuality, sin and temptation around the figure of Eve, which
would soon dominate the Christian understanding of
woman. Eve's disobedience was contrasted with Mary's
obedience, Eve brought death to the world by listening to
the serpent, Mary brought life to the world by listening
to the angel, Eve was the virgin who fell into sin, Mary was
the virgin who remained in a state of grace. Initially, this
dialectic between sin and grace, fallenness and redemption
encompassed both Mary and Eve in a complex interplay of
symbols that was intended to express the redemption of
Eve in Mary, but at the same time Eve was being constructed as the female flesh upon whose body men would
soon inscribe all their sexual fears and fantasies. Thus it
would not be long before a more rigid dualism began to
emerge, in which the subtle symbolic interchange of early
representations of Mary and Eve was forgotten. Eve,
representing all real women, became identified with the

dangers of the fallen female flesh, while Mary, representing a transcendent ideal of woman, became identified with the uniquely pure and redeemed female body.

Christianity has always taught that salvation in Christ is offered to all human beings irrespective of age, race, class, nation or gender. In the words of St Paul, 'All baptised in Christ, you have all clothed yourselves in Christ, and there are no more distinctions between Jew and Greek, slave and free, male and female, but all of you are one in Christ Jesus' (Gal. 3:27–8). This was a radical claim in the ancient world, particularly to the intellectual classes who believed that only the male citizen was fully human. Women, children, slaves and animals occupied a lower position on the hierarchy of being, and they had no direct relationship to God. I have already suggested that the idea of a union between the divine and the material world in Christ was an impossible concept for a culture that saw matter as inherently corrupt, but even for those who accepted the possibility of the human body being resurrected in a state of perfect union with God, it would have to be a male body. The female body, associated with animality rather than with divinity, could not be granted a space in heaven, and if women were to be resurrected at all, it must be as men. Although the early Church ostensibly rejected this belief, that rejection was by no means unambiguous, and even today the Catholic Church's resistance to women's ordination is rooted in an ancient uncertainty about the status of the female body in the order of   salvation.

The eastern and western Church developed two different ways of understanding the significance of the material world that continue to inform their understanding of sexual difference. These are based on the two stories of creation in Genesis 1 and Genesis 2. The first story is in fact chronologically later and was probably written after the Babylonian exile, since it is influenced by Babylonian creation myths. This tells of the simultaneous creation of male and female in the image of God: 'God created man in the image of himself, in the image of God he created him, male and female he created them' (Gen. 1:27). The Greek thinkers of the eastern Church, particularly Origen and Gregory of Nyssa, argued that this is the first stage in creation and it refers only to the human soul or reason, since God is spirit and not body, so the human body cannot be made in the image of God. The second story in Genesis 2:22, in which Eve is created from Adam's rib, was interpreted as the second stage in creation. For Origen this second creation happened after the fall, and therefore matter is inherently contaminated by sin. Although the Church rejected this idea, Orthodox Christianity retains the belief that matter, including the human body, is a secondary feature of creation. Our sexuality is not intrinsic to our being but is contingent upon the coming of death into the world. In a world in which we die we must also procreate, but in a world where death has been done away with, sexuality too becomes superfluous. Thus Orthodox theology in theory attaches no great significance to sexual difference. We were not originally created as sexual beings, and in the resurrection we will be free of our sexual characteristics. That is why, in the very early Church, the virgin body – male but especially female – had particular symbolic power. It was an affirmation of the triumph of life over death, and of the integrity and wholeness of the redeemed human being. Only later, from about the fifth century, did this become more fully identified with the rejection of sex as inherently sinful and unspiritual.

Some feminist thinkers such as Kari Elisabeth Børresen and Ruether see potential in this theological vision, since it attaches no fundamental meaning to the difference between the sexes, and therefore it cannot be used to

defend a sexual hierarchy in which one sex is closer to God
or reflects the divine image more faithfully than the
other.[2] However, they also point out that the philosophical
belief in the superiority of the male prevailed in spite of
this, so that there was still a tendency to associate the
non-sexual, redeemed body with the male. This meant
that in the early Church, being male was the ideal for both
sexes, and it was the male body and masculine virtues that
most powerfully represented the perfection of the human
in Christ. Barbara Newman identifies two early models of
Christian womanhood – the *virgo* and the *virago*.[3] The
virgo was the virginal woman who, recognizing the weakness and tendency towards sin associated with her sex,
sought to live a modest and restrained life through withdrawal from society. The *virago* was the rare woman who
was able to transcend the limitations of her sex in order to
become an honorary man – to be called '*vir*', man, was
high praise for a woman, since it acknowledged that she
had acquired the virtue (a word whose root is '*vir*') that
was the mark of the good Christian. This idea was mapped
onto the female body in the practices of asceticism, by
which a woman deliberately rendered her body as unat-
tractive as possible and, through self-starvation, suppressed the natural bodily function of menstruation and
acquired a body without the curves and contours of
femaleness. Throughout the literature of the early
Church, holy women are exalted for their manliness, just
as sinful men are castigated for their femininity. Not until
the Middle Ages would femininity acquire more positive
significance, as the language of Christian spirituality
became focused on the love relationship between the
feminine soul as bride and Christ as bridegroom.

The western Church developed a different theology of
the body, primarily owing to the influence of Augustine.
With regard to sexuality, Augustine's theology of original

sin has perhaps been one of the great scourges of the western Christian tradition, and it is closely bound up with his own experiences. As a young man, Augustine was sexually promiscuous, and before his conversion to Christianity he lived with a woman (usually referred to as his concubine) who was the mother of his son. His mother arranged a more suitable marriage and he sent his mistress away, a separation that caused him deep heartache: 'The woman with whom I had been living was torn from my side as an obstacle to my marriage and this was a blow which crushed my heart to bleeding, because I loved her dearly.'[4] Jostein Gaarder's book, *Vita Brevis: A Letter to St. Augustine*, is an imaginative reconstruction of this woman's feelings as she struggles to come to terms with the ending of their relationship.[5]

For Augustine, becoming a Christian meant renouncing sex. He never married, but it seems his body was slow to get the message. It was the uncontrollability of the male erection that led Augustine to associate original sin so closely with sex. There is one part of the human body that is utterly resistant to the control of the will but seems to have a life of its own, and the sex act itself allows passion to overwhelm reason. In Augustine's view, this showed that there was something inherently sinful about sexual desire. Its association with concupiscence – lust and loss of control – suggested that this was the means by which original sin was transmitted from generation to generation in the act of conception. Indeed, according to Augustine sexual intercourse in marriage was only permissible for the purpose of procreation. An elderly or infertile couple was guilty of lust if they had sex knowing that conception was impossible, and even a fertile couple should abstain if they could. Although there was no sin in procreative sex, it simply prolonged human life on earth and delayed the coming of God's kingdom.[6]

Augustine's problem with sex led him to contemplate whether or not God intended there to be sex in Eden, so that Adam and Eve would have had intercourse even if they had not fallen. At first he believed that they would have enjoyed a perfect celibate friendship, but later in life he saw the problem in his reasoning. After all, if God had wanted to create a perfect friend and helper for Adam, he would surely have created another man? From the beginning therefore, God must have intended sex and procreation, otherwise there was no point in creating Eve. However, sex in Eden would have been an act of the will, without passion or loss of control.

Like other Christian thinkers, Augustine was deeply influenced by Greek philosophical theories, particularly those of neo-Platonism, about the make-up of the human mind and the primacy of reason and the will over emotion and desire. In his writings we see the internalization of Christian spirituality, and the beginnings of a shift from a cosmic vision of humanity's place in a redeemed creation, to a more psychological understanding of redemption. Thinkers such as Origen saw the human spirit as a micro-universe. He wrote, 'Understand that you are another universe, a universe in miniature; that in you there are sun, moon, and stars too.'[7] But for Augustine, the mind itself was the locus of the drama of salvation and the struggle for virtue, and at times his writings suggest that he saw human sexuality primarily as a metaphor for this struggle. In order for a person to live a good life, masculine wisdom and reason must prevail over feminine passion and desire, just as in the social order a man has authority over his wife. This association of masculinity with reason led him to argue that, because divine reason is the source of the image of God in humankind, man rather than woman is directly made in the image of God, while she only images God together with her husband. In other words, the human mind is godlike when it is governed by reason, just as a woman acquires godlikeness when she is united to and governed by her husband. He writes:

the woman together with her husband is the image of
God, so that the whole substance is one image. But
when she is assigned as a help-mate, a function that
pertains to her alone, then she is not the image of God;
but as far as the man is concerned, he is by himself
alone the image of God, just as fully and completely as
when he and the woman are joined together into one.[8]

The second version of creation in Genesis has from the
time of the Pauline epistles been used to defend the sexual
status quo, even although contemporary biblical scholars
such as Phyllis Trible argue that the text lends no support
to the idea of man's superiority over woman in the order of
creation.[9] For example, in the First Letter to the
Corinthians we read:

A man should certainly not cover his head, since he is
the image of God and reflects God's glory; but woman
is the reflection of man's glory. For man did not come
from woman; no, woman came from man; and man
was not created for the sake of woman, but woman
was created for the sake of man (1 Cor. 11:7–10).

Thus in a tradition that has remained virtually unchallenged since New Testament times until the advent of
feminist biblical scholarship in the twentieth century, the
men of the Church have consistently read Genesis 2 as
lending support to the idea that woman was in the beginning created as man's subordinate. Aquinas argues that,
although woman's domination by man was a consequence
of the fall, her subordination to man was a natural part of
the goodness of creation, willed by God, since the social
order depends on there being those who lead and those
who obey. In one form or another, this argument occurs in
all the texts of the great Christian theologians, Protestant

and Catholic – Augustine, Aquinas, Luther, Barth and von
Balthasar, to name but a few – and it also threads its way
through the art and literature of western culture.
Consider, for example, the following extract from Milton's
Paradise Lost:

Two of far nobler shape erect and tall,
God-like erect, with native honour clad
In naked majesty seemed lords of all,
And worthy seemed, for in their looks divine
The image of their glorious Maker shone,
Truth, wisdom, sanctitude severe and pure,
Severe but in true filial freedom placed;
Whence true authority in men; though both
Not equal, as their sex not equal seemed;
For contemplation he and valour formed,
For softness she and sweet attractive grace;
He for God only, she for God in him.
His fair large front and eye sublime declared
Absolute rule; and hyacinthine locks
Round from his parted forelock manly hung
Clust'ring, but not beneath his shoulders broad:
She as a veil down to the slender waist
Her unadornèd golden tresses wore
Dishevelled, but in wanton ringlets waved
As the vine curls her tendrils, which implied
Subjection, but required with gentle sway,
And by her yielded, by him best received,
Yielded with coy submission, modest pride,
And sweet reluctant amorous delay . . .

Milton was writing in a cultural milieu in which the
actual story of Genesis had become so overlaid by the conventions of society, that even his creative genius did not
question the sexual hierarchies attributed to it. Indeed,

one of the concerns of *Paradise Lost* is the question of
authority and obedience, including Eve's disobedience
with regard to Adam's husbandly authority over her. Thus
in the beginning, even before the fall, Milton depicts Adam
and Eve in sexual stereotypes that derive hardly anything
from the Bible and almost everything from cultural interpretations. Adam is strong, manly and authoritative, Eve
is subject to him, seductive and wanton.

But while Augustine played a significant part in establishing these stereotypes, he was not always consistent in
his arguments, and it is as if he sometimes forgets himself
and takes his own metaphorical language too literally. If
male and female sexual bodies are primarily significant as
metaphors for the image of God in the human mind, then it
is clear that women no less than men are endowed with
that image. Women, like men, are creatures of reason, made
in the image of God and intended for salvation. This might
be seen as the dualistic aspect of Augustine's thought. The
mind, not the body, is the locus of human identity and it is
where the story of each individual's salvation is played out.
As a young man Augustine had been influenced by
Manichaeism, which held that the material world was
inherently corrupt and therefore could not in any way be
identified with the divine. This suspicion of matter lingers
on in Augustine's work, particularly as far as sexuality is
concerned. But as a Christian, Augustine was also joyously
and passionately convinced that the incarnation affirmed
the goodness and value of the material world.

This insistence on the goodness of matter and the body
paradoxically makes Augustine one of the greatest cham-
pions ever of woman's place in the Christian story. As a
man of his time, he did not escape the sexual and social
stereotypes of his society. But that is only part of his theology
of woman, and the other part – the neglected part – is more
interesting and hopeful. It was Augustine who decisively

introduced into the western Church the belief that sexual difference is a feature of creation and therefore it has eternal significance. The female body had a place in God's world in the beginning, and she has a place in God's world for all eternity. Rejecting the idea of a double creation, Augustine argued that God brought the whole universe into being in a single creative act, including the creation of the male and female human being. Thus, refuting the claims of those who argued that only the male body could be resurrected, he insisted:

> a woman's sex is not a defect; it is natural. And in the resurrection it will be free of the necessity of inter-course and childbirth. However, the female organs will not subserve their former use; they will be part of a new beauty, which will not excite the lust of the beholder – there will be no lust in that life – but will arouse the praises of God for his wisdom and compassion, in that he not only created out of nothing but freed from corruption that which he had created.[10]

This idea that the female body is an end in itself, created not for its procreative and sexual functions but for the glory and praise of God, has never been fully developed in the Christian tradition. While the Catholic doctrine of the Assumption – the belief that Mary was assumed bodily into heaven at the end of her earthly life – affirms that there is indeed one female body in heaven, it is difficult to see how this is given sacramental expression in the life of the Church. A woman's body has no positive significance in the Catholic liturgy, and the only occasion on which her presence is required is at the marriage ceremony. In the late twentieth century, in response to the challenge of the women's movement and particularly to the campaign for women's ordination, this physical exclusion of the female body from the sacramental life of the Church has been given added impetus through a subtle but far-reaching transformation in the Catholic understanding of the symbolic significance of sexuality.

On the one hand, from the 1950s the Catholic doctrine of marriage began to move away from an idea of a sexual hierarchy to that of equality in difference between husband and wife. The wife is no longer understood as subordinate to her husband, but as having different roles and responsibilities associated with femininity and motherhood as opposed to masculinity and fatherhood. This ostensible shift to a more equal understanding of sexual relationships has in fact given rise to a theology of sexual difference that has deeply troubling implications for the understanding of salvation, because it raises a question as to whether or not the female flesh is truly redeemed in Christ.

Masculinity and femininity have always been understood symbolically as well as biologically in the Catholic tradition. Since the time of Augustine, the relationship between the sexes has been seen as an analogy for the relationship between God and humankind, so that man has been identified with transcendence, divinity and the spirit, and woman with immanence, humanity and the flesh, but these have been first and foremost theological relationships. Although they have spilled over into society so that the Christian social order has been modelled upon these relationships of male superiority and female subordination, in theory at least, both sexes have had access to the language of the other, to explore who they are in relation to God. I suggested above that, in the early Church, manliness was the ideal for both sexes, and there was no higher praise for a Christian woman than to be called a man. Womanliness was unambiguously associated with weakness, the flesh and sin, and this meant that the female body was a spiritual encumbrance for both women and men. Men had to resist its allures in order to seek God, and women had to transcend its demands and its frailties. Round about the twelfth century, Christian devotion began to undergo a shift in emphasis. It was then that the male soul started to describe himself as feminine in relation to Christ, so that the language of the Bride in the *Song of Songs* became the language of the soul in her longing for the Bridegroom, Christ. Clearly, this means that gendered language does not literally describe the sexual body. The relationship between language and the body is not one of biological essentialism but of metaphor and symbolism.

Biologically, male and female bodies were not believed to be essentially different. The female was, as Aquinas argued from Aristotle, 'a defective male'. Christ was male, not because that was fundamentally different from being female, but because it was the superior version of the same body. Here as elsewhere, the Catholic understanding of female embodiment is muddled and self-contradictory. Aquinas tried to reconcile Augustine's belief in the resurrection of woman with Aristotle's belief in the defectiveness of the female body, without ever quite explaining how a defective male body could become a perfect female body in its heavenly state. This kind of confusion is everywhere apparent, as soon as one tries to trace a coherent path through the different ways in which the female body has been represented theologically. Is a woman a defective male, a different incarnation, or a sexless being who shares with man a primal condition unmarked by sexual difference? Of course, these questions are ultimately unanswerable. Freud himself acknowledged that sexual difference remains a profound mystery. He refers to 'the great enigma of the biological fact of the duality of the sexes: for our knowledge it is something ultimate, it resists every attempt to trace it back to something else'.[11] But in Christianity, this enigma has translated into a muddled ideology, driven not by an authentic theological quest to decipher the signs of revelation encoded in the sexual body, but by the imperative to rationalize and perpetuate the patriarchal social order that prevailed in pre-Christian society, and that found new justification and reinforcement in the development of Christian theology.

In the late twentieth century, confronted with growing pressure to give a theological explanation for its refusal to ordain women, Catholic theology adopted a quasi-scientific approach to sexual difference that led to a much greater degree of biological literalism. Thomas Laqueur argues that the idea of a fundamental biological difference between the sexes can be traced back to the scientific revolution that began in the late seventeenth century, and that this scientific 'discovery' of sexual difference closely parallels changes in the social order.[12] I have already referred to studies that suggest a change in the philosophical understanding of female embodiment and nature in the seventeenth century, which led to the increasing privatization of women's lives and their disempowerment in the public sphere. Laqueur suggests that it is not coincidental that scientists, conditioned by their cultural environment, developed a theory of masculine activity, rationality and authority, and feminine passivity, irrationality and submissiveness, based not on social but on biological differences between the sexes. In the twentieth century, the Catholic hierarchy appropriated this idea and used it to justify the exclusion of women from the sacramental priesthood, in a way that profoundly distorts the traditional understanding of the story of redemption.

Hans Urs von Balthasar, arguably the most significant influence on contemporary Catholic doctrine in the area of sexuality, borrows these scientific ideas to bolster his insistence that men and women are essentially and fundamentally different, and that it is a violation of a woman's

natural femininity to seek ordination. He claims that 'The
male body is male throughout, right down to each cell of
which it consists, and the female body is utterly female;
and this is also true of their whole empirical experience
and ego-consciousness.'[13] Nevertheless, this does not prevent him from insisting repeatedly that all human beings,
male as well as female, are feminine in relation to God,
because God is the active, masculine principle in creation,
and femininity signifies the receptivity and openness of the
human creature to divine life, perfectly exemplified in
Mary. This idea of symbolic femininity associated with
both sexes also appears in the writings of John Paul II,
who, in his apostolic letter on the dignity of women,
Mulieris Dignitatem, writes:

> all human beings – both women and men – are called
> through the Church, to be the 'Bride' of Christ, the
> Redeemer of the world. In this way 'being the bride',
> and thus the 'feminine' element, becomes a symbol of
> all that is 'human', according to the words of Paul:
> 'There is neither male nor female; for you are all one
> in Christ Jesus' (Gal 3:28).[14]

In other words, the Catholic theology of sexual difference is now utterly confused, in a way that affects the doctrine of salvation. On the one hand, femininity continues
to operate just as it always has done, to symbolize the relationship between the human and the divine in a way that
is relevant for both sexes. Thus men can perform both
masculine and feminine roles in the sacramental life of the
Church. As priests, they represent the Bridegroom, Christ,
and as worshippers they represent the Bride, the Church.
This is explained in the 1976 Vatican document on the
sacramental priesthood, *Inter Insigniores*, which argues
that the nuptial symbolization of the relationship between

Christ and the Church requires that a man represents
Christ as 'the author of the Covenant, the Bridegroom and
Head of the Church.'[15] The document acknowledges that
the priest also represents the Church, and so the priestly
role could arguably be performed by a woman. However, it
insists that this is not possible, because if the priest represents the Church which is the Body of Christ, 'it is precise-
ly because he first represents Christ himself, who is the
Head and Shepherd of the Church'.[16] I have analysed these
arguments in some depth elsewhere,[17] so here I would just
reiterate the point that women have now been excluded in
a more radical way than ever before from their relationship
to the humanity of Christ. The doctrine of salvation has
always insisted that we are redeemed because Christ took
human flesh, not because he took male flesh, and implicit in
this has been the understanding that the flesh of Christ
incorporates both sexes. For Augustine, Mary's role in the
incarnation was evidence that both male and female bodies
participated in and benefited from salvation. He argues:

> just as death came to us through a woman, life was
> born to us through a woman. And so, by the nature of
> both one and the other, that is to say, female and male,
> the devil was vanquished and put to torture, he who
> had rejoiced in their downfall. It would have con-
> tributed little to his punishment if those two natures
> had been delivered in us without our being delivered
> by both of them.[18]

Caroline Walker Bynum, in her study of medieval writers,
identifies 'several separate strands on which medieval mystics drew in identifying woman with flesh and Christ's flesh
with the female'.[19] These included theological ideas that
associated the male with the spirit and the female with the
flesh, and also ideas associated with the sinless flesh of Mary

as the one who gave Christ his human body. So although the female flesh has consistently been viewed with suspicion even as Christian concepts of femininity have changed over the centuries, there have in the past been many ways in which women have been able to appropriate for themselves the shifting gender symbolism of the Christian tradition to affirm their place in the story of salvation.

Today, however, the claim that Christ's masculinity is an essential feature of his divinity, in a way that precludes women from representing Christ on the altar, leads to two conclusions that must surely be deemed heretical in terms of the Christian tradition. First, it posits an essential relationship between God and masculinity, which violates the Christian insistence that God is beyond all human characteristics, including those of gender. Second, it suggests that the female flesh forms no part of the incarnation of God in Christ, and therefore neither can it be part of the resurrection of the body in Christ.

The theological tradition offers feminist theologians two possible lines of argument to resist this development. On the one hand, it could be argued with eastern Christianity that this represents a misunderstanding of the nature of sexual difference. Sexuality is not an essential aspect of the human being, and it does not constitute the image of God in humankind. The sexual body can therefore have no liturgical or sacramental significance, in so far as it plays no part in the divine image or in the symbolization of the world to come. Alternatively, it could be argued with Augustine that our sexual bodies are endowed with eternal significance, and therefore both male and female bodies are created for the glory of God. This would entail going beyond Augustine's theological vision, conditioned as it is by the sexual stereotypes and hierarchies of the ancient world, to ask in what ways the female body might have its own unique form of sacramentality and priesthood, so as to make Catholic worship a more complete and fulfilled expression of our faith in the world to come. But I want to probe more deeply into the puzzle as to why, throughout the Christian tradition, men have been so reluctant to let go of the ancient sexual stereotypes that have cramped the Christian understanding of the relationship between God and humankind in the redeemed and equal community of the Church. Why did the Christian faith, with all its early potential to become a story of reconciling peace for all creation, so quickly mutate into yet another oppressive religion of control and abusive power, with so much of its destructive energy focused on the female body and sexuality?

1 Carol Shields, *Unless* (London and New York: Fourth Estate, 2002), p. 179.
2 See Kari Elisabeth Børresen, 'God's Image, Man's Image? Patristic Interpretations of Gen. 1.27 and 1 Cor. 11.7' in Børresen (ed.), *The Image of God – Gender Models in Judaeo-Christian Tradition* (Minneapolis: Fortress Press, 1995); Rosemary Radford Ruether, 'Misogynism and Virginal Feminism in the Fathers of the Church' in Ruether (ed.), *Religion and Sexism – Images of Woman in the Jewish and Christian Traditions* (New York: Simon & Schuster, 1974).
3 Barbara Newman, *From Virile Woman to WomanChrist: Studies in Medieval Religion and Literature* (Philadelphia: University of Pennsylvania Press, 1995).
4 Augustine, *Confessions*, trans. R. S. Pine-Coffin (Harmondsworth: Penguin Books, 1961), Bk VI, 15, p. 131.
5 Jostein Gaarder, *Vita Brevis: A Letter to St. Augustine* (London: Phoenix, 1998).
6 For Augustine's writings on marriage, virginity and sexuality, see Kari Elisabeth Børresen, *Subordination and Equivalence: The Nature and Role of Woman in Augustine and Thomas Aquinas* (Kampen: Kok Pharos Publishing House, 1995); Elizabeth A. Clark, *St. Augustine on Marriage and Sexuality* (Washington DC: Catholic University of America Press, 1996).
7 Origen, Fifth Homily on Leviticus, 2, quoted in Olivier Clément, *The Roots of Christian Mysticism*, trans. Theodore Berkeley, O.C.S.O. (London: New City, 1997), p. 78.
8 Augustine, The Trinity, trans. Stephen McKenna, C.S.S.R, *The Fathers of the Church*, a new translation (Washington DC: The Catholic University of America Press, 1963), Bk 12, Ch. 7, n. 10.
9 See Phyllis Trible, *God and the Rhetoric of Sexuality* (Philadelphia: Fortress Press, 1978).
10 Augustine, *Concerning the City of God against the Pagans* [1467], ed. David Knowles, trans. Henry Bettenson (London: Penguin Books, 1981), Bk 22, Ch. 17, p. 1057.

11 Sigmund Freud, *An Outline of Psycho-Analysis* [1938, unfinished], trans. James Strachey (London: The Hogarth Press and the Institute of Psycho-Analysis, 1949), p. 55.

12 See Thomas Laqueur, *Making Sex: Body and Gender from the Greeks to Freud* (Cambridge MA and London: Harvard University Press, 1992).

13 Hans Urs von Balthasar, *Theo-Drama: Theological Dramatic Theory, Vol. 2: The Dramatis Personae: Man in God*, trans. Graham Harrison (San Francisco: Ignatius Press, 1990), p. 365.

14 John Paul II, *Mulieris Dignitatem: Apostolic letter on the dignity and vocation of women on the occasion of the Marian year* (London: Catholic Truth Society, 1988), p. 94, n. 25.

15 *Inter Insigniores: Declaration on the Admission of Women to the Ministerial Priesthood*, 15 October 1976, in Austin Flannery, O.P. (gen.ed.), *Vatican Council II, Volume 2, More Postconciliar Documents* (Collegeville: The Liturgical Press, 1982), p. 340.

16 Ibid., 341.

17 See Beattie, *God's Mother, Eve's Advocate*, pp. 71–81.

18 Augustine, De agone Christiano, 22, 24, CSEL.41, p. 124, quoted in Børresen, *Subordination and Equivalence*, p. 75.

19 Caroline Walker Bynum, *Fragmentation and Redemption: Essays on Gender and the Human Body in Medieval Religion* (New York: Zone Books, 1992), p. 206.

6
Woman and the Feminine Soul

The Woman
So beautiful – God himself quailed
At her approach: the long body curved
like the horizon. Why had he made
her so? How would it be, she said,
leaning towards him, if instead of
quarrelling over it, we divided it
between us? You can have all the credit
for its invention, if you will leave the ordering
of it to me. He looked into her
eyes and saw far down the bones
of the generations that would navigate
by those great stars, but the pull of it
was too much. Yes, he thought, give me their minds'
tribute, and what they do with their bodies
is not my concern. He put his hand in his side
and drew out the thorn for the letting
of the ordained blood and touched her with
it. Go, he said. They shall come to you for ever
with their desire, and you shall bleed for them in
return.

R. S. Thomas[1]

There has always been a tension, a contradiction even,
between the Christian belief that men and women are both
fully human and fully equal in the eyes of God, and the
development of a theology that has upheld the sexual and
social hierarchies of patriarchal society. On the one hand,
the Christian belief in sexual equality – which was unique

to Christianity in the ancient world – created the conditions in which our modern concepts of equality and justice have come into being. On the other hand, Christianity has cultivated a denigratory and even hostile attitude towards women, because of its profound suspicion of the sexual body and its almost sado-masochistic celebration of the suffering body. Although this has affected the self-perception and spiritual practices of both men and women, it has been focused in a particularly intense way on female embodiment. Scholars such as Bynum and Jantzen see a greater preoccupation with the body and a greater tendency towards extreme practices of asceticism in the writings of female mystics than of male mystics.[2]

There is no one answer to the dilemma of Christian misogyny, but the explanation must lie at least partly in the related influences of patriarchy and pollution in the formation of religious traditions. Patriarchy in its different cultural and historical manifestations would appear to be the most widespread form of social organization. It refers to social structures mediated in descending hierarchies of fatherhood, from concepts of divinity down through kings and priests, male authority figures and family relationships in which the father is the head of the house. Although this system has largely disintegrated with regard to the formal structures of western society, its legacy continues in a culture that still privileges men over women in its political, institutional and economic worlds.

Some romantic feminists suggest that ancient cultures were matriarchal, and they make extravagant claims about the social harmony and closeness to nature inherent in such societies. However, the existence of female deity figures in archaeological remains does not necessarily point to matriarchal social structures. One need only think of the goddesses of Hinduism or the predominance of devotion to the Virgin Mary in Latin America, to realize that religious devotion to feminine figures does not necessarily translate into the elevation of women in society.

Catholic Christianity has been and still is a classically patriarchal institution. God the Father is worshipped through Jesus the Son, whose earthly ministry is exercised through exclusively male hierarchies of popes, bishops, priests and deacons, holding roles of fatherly authority over the religious community depicted in feminine imagery. As the maternal feminine figure in this hierarchy, Mary is subordinate to God the Father and to Jesus the Son, both of whom are at various times referred to as her husband in Catholic writings. Around the edges of this traditional family hovers the Holy Spirit, described as feminine in some of the writings of the early Church, but resolutely masculine since the fifth century. Although the early Church had the potential to challenge and transform the patriarchal structures of Roman society, it internalized them and made them part of its own understanding of the unchanging nature of personal relationships, both human and divine. Thus after the conversion of Rome in the fourth century, Christian concepts of gender became increasingly more solidified around a patriarchal ideology, underpinned and justified by belief in a Father God invested with the characteristics of idealized masculinity.

Virginia Burrus, in her fine study of early Christian theology, argues that Christianity's fundamental theological concepts were worked out at a time of crisis for the concept of masculinity in the Roman empire. During the era of persecution under the Romans, the early Church was a feminized collective, in so far as it lacked institutional power and its members, men and women alike, occupied positions of vulnerability and exclusion in the social order, in a culture in which the loss of masculinity was the ultimate threat to the male citizen's sense of dignity and self-esteem. Thus early Christian language

encompassed femininity, echoing 'the feminized virility of
the wounded hero'[3] found in Platonism and the literature of
the early Roman Empire. But with the conversion and fall
of Rome, the Church's leaders had to assume masculine
roles of leadership, authority and public office, and Burrus
demonstrates convincingly how the need to negotiate a
Christian concept of masculinity consistent with these
demands affected both the theology and the anthropology
of the Christian faith in profound and enduring ways.
Reading the texts of three Christian thinkers – Athanasius
of Alexandria, Gregory of Nyssa and Ambrose of Milan – in
engagement with Irigaray, Burrus argues that the doctrine
of the Trinity formulated at the Council of Nicea played a
pivotal role in the construction of the Christian understanding of manhood. Belief in a disembodied, transcendent
masculine divinity reflected the ultimate qualities of the
ideal man whom the Church's leaders aspired to be, while
femininity became encoded within this symbolic framework
as an expression of the weakness, vulnerability, and bodily and
emotional needs that of course these men still experienced.

It is impossible to summarize the rich complexity of
Burrus's readings of the Church Fathers here, but her
study shows the extent to which the psychological relationship between masculinity and God operates at the
deepest level of theological language and symbolism. She
writes, 'The fourth-century doctrine of a transcendent God
who is Father, Son, and Holy Spirit was inextricably inter-
twined with the particular late-antique claims for masculinity.'[4] However, Burrus also sees this as an inherently
unstable concept, because the ever-present threat of
maternal femininity encompassed within it in various
ways invites new readings and interpretations, so that
'what is disavowed, suppressed, or dismissed as excessive
in Christian discourse – seemingly so much "nothing" –
provides excellent material with which to create. ... [F]or a

humanity said to be created in the image of God, ancient theology is a gift that keeps on giving.'[5]

This repressed potential of maternal femininity brings me to the next possible explanation for Christianity's denigration of the female body, and that is the concept of purity and pollution. If a partial explanation for the subordination of women in the Church lies in the pervasive influence of a patriarchal social order and in distorted readings of the story of creation and the fall in Genesis 2 and 3 that have persistently been used to lend divine justification to this order, this does not explain the depth of revulsion and dread that Christian men have exhibited towards the female body in their writings and devotions over the centuries. It is one thing to find security in authority structures and stable social hierarchies, but it is another to live one's life in a state of constant avoidance of half the human race lest one's spirit be contaminated. To explain this phenomenon, I think we need to consider the deep psychological and religious impulses that lead to the female body being perceived as a particularly dangerous source of pollution.

I have suggested earlier that Tertullian was one of the first Christian thinkers to identify all women with Eve, in a way that has led to the denigration of the female body throughout the Christian tradition. However, like Augustine, Tertullian was a man of his time who also struggled bravely against the ideas of his time, particularly with regard to beliefs about the inferiority of matter in general and the female body in particular. Tertullian argued passionately against those who refused to accept that Christ could have been born of a woman without the pollution of his divine nature.[6] Augustine, although less colourful in his rhetoric than Tertullian, also argued against the idea that the female flesh was a source of pollution to the divine spirit. He asks his opponents, 'Suppose I am not able to show why he should choose to be born of a woman; you must still show me what he ought to avoid in a woman.'[7] He goes on to argue that, although Christ could have been born without a woman, he chose to honour both sexes in the incarnation. He imagines Christ saying:

> To show you that it's not any creature of God that is bad, but that it's crooked pleasures that distort them, in the beginning when I made man, I made them male and female. I don't reject and condemn any creature that I have made. Here I am, born a man, born of a woman. So I don't reject any creature I have made, but I reject and condemn sins, which I didn't make. Let each sex take note of its proper honor, and each confess its iniquity, and each hope for salvation.[8]

The very fact that for the first five centuries of the Christian era, such key thinkers as Tertullian and Augustine had to defend female embodiment against charges of inherent pollution and defilement, suggests how widespread such beliefs were. However, despite their efforts, the lingering terror of female pollution overwhelmed the promise of the early Church, and women have occupied a position in Christianity not dissimilar from their position in many other religions and cultures. Christianity's unique celebration of the goodness of creation and the divinization of the human flesh in Christ soon yielded to primal fears with regard to the mortality, flux and dependence of the body, and these accumulated around the body of woman in a way that eradicated any sense of her glory before God. Only the Virgin Mary, purged of any trace of the corruption associated with sexual intercourse, childbirth and death, became a safe feminine object of devotion while her opposite, Eve, became the bearer of all the sexual temptations and sins of humankind. Beginning with Eve, woman has been perceived as having the power to deflect man from his orientation towards godliness, and to lure him into the sins of the flesh which he experiences as alienation from the transcendent perfection of God, in whose image he believes himself to be made. Through the ages, Christian men have urged women to be modest, humble and self-effacing, to shun the outward beauty of the body in order to cultivate the inner beauty of the soul. In other words, the problem of sexual temptation has been located, not in the male body but in the adorned female body, and it is woman who is responsible for seducing the man and leading him into corruption and impurity.

The stories of history and culture are marked by themes of purity and pollution, with the polluting potential of the female body being a recurring belief that transcends the particularities of religions and contexts. It is found in Hinduism, Buddhism, African traditions, Judaism, Islam and Christianity. Some scholars associate this with a primal fear of the power of blood. The bleeding woman is a symbol of both fertility and death. Blood has awesome religious potency, and sacrificial rituals are carefully controlled occasions – almost universally administered by male priests – when blood is shed to appease the gods. On these occasions, blood has sacred power. But blood is also associated with man's lack of control, with the fearful chaos of violence, and also with the threat of the female body. In Mary Douglas's anthropological study of purity and pollution, she argues that cultural definitions of the impure vary, but they are always associated with things being out of place.[9] In religious sacrifice, blood has a rightful place, but for a woman to perform the sacrifice is to introduce disorder and the fear of chaos into the ritual. Her bleeding is out of control – it is out of place in a religious context – and therefore the female sacrificial priest creates symbolic confusion. Women's bodies bleed naturally, and this threatens the cultic significance of the controlled shedding of sacrificial blood. It means something very different for a woman to say, 'This is my body, this is my blood', and for a man to say, 'This is my body, this is my blood.'[10] The former brings us close to nature, close to the cycles and patterns of our bodily selves that remind us that we are earthlings, creatures who share the animality of the natural world. The latter implies an act of mind over matter, of conscious martyrdom willingly chosen, of blood shed not naturally but deliberately and purposefully, for some higher ideal. Whether on the cross or on the battlefield, the Christian imagination has had a morbid proclivity for the glorious shedding of men's blood. And while it has never accommodated the fertile, sexual, bleeding female body into its symbolic life – the Virgin Mary, according to tradition, conceived through her ear and gave birth through her side, without loss of either her virginity or her purity – Catholic hagiographies abound with stories of tortured and martyred female bodies whose blood has been shed by men. In other words, women's blood too becomes holy, when it is lifted out of its natural context of fertility and incorporated into the violent symbolics of martyrdom.[11]

But if female bloodshed is one possible explanation as to why women's bodies represent a source of fear to men, psychoanalysis offers another explanation.[12] Fear of pollution, bodily fluids, birth and death are closely associated. In the Levitical codes of the Old Testament, semen, blood, milk, the maternal body after childbirth and the corpse are all sources of pollution. For the people of Israel, pollution meant loss of identity. They derived their identity as God's chosen people through their separation from the surrounding Canaanite cults, and this separation was sustained through purity laws. To be impure was also to lose the mark of difference, to have one's identity tainted by otherness, and to risk being absorbed into that otherness. De Beauvoir was the first to identify woman as the other of

man in her groundbreaking book, *The Second Sex*.[13] Since
then, volumes have been written by academics across all
disciplines concerned with the question of the other, so that
the expression is acquiring the status of a cliché.
Notwithstanding this caution, the recognition of otherness
has been an important insight as the intellectual structures
of the modern world disintegrate. Through acknowledgement of the other, the autonomous western man of reason
is shown to be not the universal representative of the
human race which he believed himself to be, but to be a
narrowly defined and repressed individual whose identity is
preserved through a sustained struggle to avoid the pollution of the other – the foreigner, the native, the woman.[14]

Man knows who he is by knowing who he is not – he is
not woman. But his identity is surrounded and threatened
by womanly presences. The womb that nurtured him into
being was also a tomb, because it was a time when he was
not one, not separate, and had no identity, just as in death
he will lose his identity, his oneness, his separation from
nature. And the female body itself gapes at him, luring him
in, arousing his desire so that he becomes conscious of his
vulnerability and his dependence. He is afraid that the
woman will swallow him up if he enters her, and yet enter
her he must because his whole being is drawn to her. Thus
she reminds him of the fragility of his sense of self, the
impossibility of remaining spiritually and intellectually
free of the body, nature and dependence on another. If he
is to transcend his natural inclinations, his passions, emotions and vulnerabilities, if he is to become a man, he must
do everything he can to keep his identity secure from the
taint of womanliness, the other, the body.

This is the haunted psyche of oppositions and struggles
– identity or otherness, spirit or flesh, control or desire –
that Christianity has allowed to flourish within its symbolic
and social worlds. It is a fear that marks the texts of

masculinity from the twentieth century back to the time of
the church fathers. Consider, for example, the attitude
towards female sexuality implicit in the following passage,
in which von Balthasar imagines Christ's sexual conquest
of his Bride, the Church. Von Balthasar's 'Christ' admits to
'the temptation of delivering myself up to the obscure
chaos of a body, of plunging below the shiny surface of the
flesh . . . this simmering darkness, opposed to the Father's
light'.[15] He continues,

> I dared to enter the body of my Church, the deadly
> body which *you* are. For the spirit is mortal only with-
> in its own body. And so, from now on, we are no longer
> two but, together, only one flesh which loves itself and
> which struggles and wages battle with itself even to
> the point of death. . . . (Never has woman made more
> desperate resistance!)[16]

For von Balthasar, Christ becomes incarnate through a
violent struggle in which the transcendence of 'the
Father's light' is pitted against the 'obscure chaos' and the
'simmering darkness' of the female body. Sexuality is not a
mutual expression of tenderness and love, but a deadly
battle between the spirit and the flesh, in which the male
spirit, seduced and lured towards the female flesh, must
ultimately reassert its power through rape and conquest.
Again and again, men's spiritual writings express this
sense of conflict between the desires of their own flesh, projected onto the female body as the source of temptation
and sin, and the threat that female sexuality poses to their
identification with the transcendent male God. But for von
Balthasar as for generations before him, this struggle is
complicated by the fact that the soul, male or female, is
feminine, so the man's desire to overwhelm and rape the
woman is arguably a veiled expression of his own desire to

be overwhelmed and raped by Christ, in a sado-masochistic spirituality of warped desire fed by violence. John Donne writes:

> Batter my heart, three-person'd God; for, you
> As yet but knocke, breathe, shine, and seeke to mend;
> That I may rise, and stand, o'erthrow mee,'and bend
> Your force, to breake, blowe, burn and make me new.
> I, like an unsurpt towne, to'another due,
> Labour to'admit you, but Oh, to no end,
> Reason your viceroy in mee, mee should defend,
> But is captiv'd, and proves weake or untrue.
> Yet dearely'I love you,'and would be loved faine,
> But am betroth'd unto your enemie;
> Divorce mee,'untie, or breake that knot againe,
> Take mee to you, imprison mee, for I
> Except you'enthrall mee, never shall be free,
> Nor ever chast, except you ravish mee.

These male spiritual fantasies resonate with the idea that women are 'asking for it', that the raped woman is not really a victim of violence but one who secretly longs to be defeated, conquered, broken and ravished. From this perspective, the Christian tradition is no less problematic than the modern media in its stereotypes and assumptions about women. Indeed, some feminists would argue that the denigration and objectification of the female body perpetuated by the modern media industry is simply a continuation by other means of Christianity's age-old war against the female body. Susan Griffin, in her influential study of pornography, argues that the pornographer shares the hatred of women's bodies that was inculcated into western culture by the church fathers.[17]

I referred earlier to the change in Christian spirituality, usually associated with the writings of Bernard of

Clairvaux in the twelfth century, in which men began to
assume the *persona* of the Bride of the *Song of Songs* in
their devotions. But if femininity acquired more positive
symbolic significance as a result of this, the female body
became even more acutely perceived as a source of sin.
The fourteenth-century English mystic, Richard Rolle,
when he first had the vocation to run off and be a hermit,
caused something of a stir when he stole two of his
sister's dresses to make himself a hermit's outfit. A
hagiography tells how his sister, upon finding him, cried
out, "'My brother is mad! My brother is mad!"
Whereupon he drove her from him with threats, and fled
himself at once without delay, lest he should be seized
upon by his friends and acquaintances.'[18] In *The Fire of
Love*, Rolle describes his mystical experiences in colourful
language. Like other mystics of the time, he expresses his
soul's love for Christ in erotic terms, with frequent
allusions to the *Song of Songs*:

> The soul that is truly separated from vice ... enjoys
> quite remarkable pleasure because she is in some way
> experiencing the delight of her Beloved's love. . . . Now
> is the time when she demands her Spouse's most gra-
> cious lips, and his sweetest kiss. 'All earthly things
> I despise,' she cries, 'I know how much I love my
> Beloved, I am aware of his most wonderful comfort, I
> yearn for his sweetness, I am not going to fail now that
> the greatest temptations have been put behind me.
> Love is making me bold to summon my Beloved that
> he might comfort me, come unto me, and *kiss me with
> the kiss of his mouth*. For the more I am raised above
> earthly thoughts the more fully do I enjoy the pleasure
> I long for; the more carnal longings are banished, so
> much the more truly do the eternal ones flare up. Let
> him kiss me and refresh me with his sweet love; let

him hold me tight and kiss me on the mouth, else I die; let him pour his grace into me, that I may grow in love.'[19]

This passage implies a highly eroticized love affair between the feminized soul and Christ. But what makes possible this appropriation of the language of feminine desire? – spiritual transcendence, and the repudiation of the flesh, or, to be more precise, the female flesh. Rolle says later that 'carnal love inevitably excites temptations . . . and hinders fervent love for Christ'. He goes on,

a man who honestly wants to love Christ must not let his imagination toy with the love of women. When women love, they love without reserve, because they do not know how to restrain their manner of loving. On the other hand loving them can be a very tricky and prickly business! . . . Loving women upsets the balance, disturbs the reason, changes wisdom to folly, estranges the heart from God, takes the soul captive, and subjects it to demons! And he who looks at a woman with natural affection yet not with lustful desire finds he is unable to keep free from illicit urges or unclean thoughts. Often enough he feels in himself the stain of filth and even may take pleasure in the thought of developing it.

Womanly beauty leads many astray. Desire for it can sometimes subvert even righteous hearts, so that what began in spirit ends up in flesh. So beware of entering into conversation with a woman just because she is lovely. You will be caught by the poisonous disease of pleasure, and, knowingly deceived, you will set about implementing your dirty thoughts. Fool that you are, you will allow yourself to be taken captive by your enemies. Be wise then, and flee from women. Do not ever think about them, because even if a woman is

good, the devil's attack and his insinuations, the
attraction of her beauty, and the weakness of your
flesh can beguile your will beyond measure.[20]

Rolle is a particularly flamboyant writer, but he offers a
vivid illustration of a tendency that marks the texts and
practices of Catholic male spirituality. The man of faith
finds himself caught in a dilemma. The Christian dread of
homoeroticism means that if the male love affair with
Christ is to find erotic expression, it must use the language
of heterosexual love even if, for example with the poetry of
St John of the Cross, homosexual desire might lie very
close to the surface. So the celibate man needs the female
body to provide the metaphors for his love for Christ. She
is the raw material for his spiritual fantasies. But he must
also resist the real female body as that which can lure him
away from Christ through the power of his own sexuality.
So we have in the Christian faith the separation between
the female flesh identified with carnal desire and lust, and
the romantic ideal of feminine desire identified with the
man's spiritual relationship with Christ. Thus the play of
desire between woman and man is displaced and becomes
projected onto the man's longing for God in the feminized
rhetoric of prayer and devotion. This is part of the phenomenon that Michel Foucault refers to in his analysis of
western attitudes towards sexuality. He writes that

the Christian pastoral also sought to produce specific
effects on desire, by the mere fact of transforming it –
fully and deliberately – into discourse: effects of mastery and detachment, to be sure, but also an effect of
spiritual reconversion, of turning back to God, a physical effect of blissful suffering from feeling in one's
body the pangs of temptation and the love that resists
it. This is the essential thing: that Western man has

been drawn for three centuries to the task of telling everything concerning his sex; that since the classical age there has been a constant optimization and an increasing valorization of the discourse on sex; and that this carefully analytical discourse was meant to yield multiple effects of displacement, intensification, reorientation, and modification of desire itself.[21]

Rolle's writing does indeed suggest 'a physical effect of blissful suffering from feeling in one's body the pangs of temptation and the love that resists it.' But what also becomes apparent in Rolle is that the 'mastery and detachment' that enable this transformation of desire relate specifically to a man's relationships with and attitudes towards women.

Underlying all these texts is the idea of purity and pollution, associated with divine transcendence and female embodiment respectively. This is despite the fact that one of the greatest transformations that Christianity brought about in its relationship to the Jewish religion was the rejection of purity laws, and the insistence that purity and pollution are questions of grace and sin, not of contact with forbidden and permitted substances.[22]

It is against this background that Augustine must be read, as one who might have taken the Church down a different road if his positive writings on the female body had been attended to, rather than his negative writings on sex and original sin. In the men of his time, Augustine confronted ideas very similar to those of von Balthasar and Rolle, and he vehemently resisted their pathological dread of the female body, even if his failure to make peace with his own sexuality has had such a negative influence on the Christian tradition.

This is the legacy that modern women still struggle with, and it is a struggle epitomized in the pages of

Cosmopolitan. On the one hand, femininity is a transcendent ideal of perfection – a manufactured and commodified body that bears little resemblance to the living realities of the female flesh. On the other hand, real women have no voice with which to offer a different, more authentic account of women's embodied personhood as a source of dignity, meaning and worth. If the men of God invested the female body with all their sexual anxieties and robbed her of her capacity to image God, the men of Mammon have exploited that culture of denigration by using it to position women in a constant state of inadequacy and shame, perpetuated now not by spiritual fantasies of idealized femininity but by consumerist fantasies of the female body as a marketable commodity.

It is in this context that women theologians seek to reintroduce questions of God and personhood into a society that has forgotten the meaning of such words. Like Wollstonecraft, we too are situated on the cusp of an era. Wollstonecraft lived at the dawn of modernity in an age when she could still speak about God, the Gospels and the Christian faith with confidence that her readers would share her premises, however vehemently they might disagree with her interpretations and arguments. But such language is now the preserve only of a religious minority. It does not feature in secular feminism, and it certainly makes no appearance in the pages of glossy magazines. If Wollstonecraft lived at the end of the Christian era and the beginning of the modern era, today we live at the end of the modern era and the beginning of something as yet unknown and unnamed, which is inadequately referred to as postmodernism.

We do not step lightly over these thresholds. We always bring with us the traditions, cultures and histories that have shaped us and told us who we are, individually and collectively. Modernism taught us to reject the past and its claims upon us. We were encouraged to turn towards a future that was bright with promise, if only we could shed the encumbrances of religion and tradition. But we cannot do that. Psychoanalysis reveals the extent to which human beings are constituted through time. Our identities are not given but acquired through painful and prolonged childhood struggles that we carry with us through adult life. In the same way, cultures do not just happen, and we cannot reinvent the worlds we inhabit. We are creatures and communities of memory and history. So now, as the last hopes of the modern worldview fade, we find ourselves confronted once again by questions of meaning, truth, identity and justice, and today it is often women who are asking these questions in the most urgent and persistent ways.

So far, I have explored the Christian tradition regarding women primarily from a Catholic perspective. In the next chapter, however, I want to consider the alternatives offered by Protestantism, in the context of the Bible and its potential for feminist re-readings.

[1] R.S. Thomas, 'The Woman'. Originally published in R.S. Thomas, *Frequencies* (London: Macmillan, 1978). © Kunjana Thomas, 2001.

[2] See Caroline Walker Bynum, *Holy Feast and Holy Fast: The Religious Significance of Food to Medieval Women* (Berkeley, CA and London: University of California Press, 1987); Bynum, *Fragmentation and Redemption*; Grace Jantzen, *Power, Gender and Christian Mysticism* (Cambridge: Cambridge University Press, 1995).

[3] Virginia Burrus, *'Begotten not Made': Conceiving Manhood in Late Antiquity* (Stanford, CA: Stanford University Press, 2000), p. 6.

[4] Ibid., p. 189.

[5] Ibid., p. 193.

[6] See Beattie, *God's Mother, Eve's Advocate*, pp. 96–8.

[7] Augustine, 'Sermon 51' in *Sermons 51–94 on the New Testament*, trans. and notes Edmund Hill, O.P., *The Works of Saint Augustine – A Translation for the 21st Century* under the auspices of the Augustinian Heritage Institute, 1991, III, 3, p. 21.

[8] Ibid., p. 22.

[9] Mary Douglas, *Purity and Danger: An Analysis of the Concepts of Pollution and Taboo* (London and New York: Routledge, 1996).

10 See the more detailed discussion of this in Beattie, God's Mother, Eve's Advocate, pp. 194–208.

11 I am indebted to Alison Green for helping me to develop some of these ideas during my supervision of her dissertation at Wesley College, Bristol in 2001.

12 See especially Julia Kristeva, *Powers of Horror – An Essay on Abjection*, trans. Leon S. Roudiez (New York: Columbia University Press, 1982).

13 See Simone de Beauvoir, *The Second Sex* [1949], trans. H. M. Parshley (Harmondsworth: Penguin Books, 1972).

14 For a more detailed exploration of these ideas, see Julia Kristeva, *Strangers to Ourselves*, trans. Leon S. Roudiez (Hemel Hempstead: Harvester, 1991).

15 Hans Urs von Balthasar, *Heart of the World*, trans. Erasmo S. Leiva (San Francisco: Ignatius Press, 1980), pp. 195–6.

16 Ibid., p. 196.

17 See Susan Griffin, *Pornography and Silence* (London: Women's Press, 1981).

18 Richard Rolle, *The Fire of Love*, trans. Clifton Wolters (Harmondsworth: Penguin Books, 1972), p. 13.

19 Ibid., p. 125.

20 Ibid., p. 136.

21 Michel Foucault, *The History of Sexuality*, Vol. 1, trans. Robert Hurley (Harmondsworth: Penguin Books, 1990), p. 23.

22 See L. W. Countryman, *Dirt, Greed and Sex* (London: SCM Press, 1989). The foregoing discussion is developed in Tina Beattie, 'The Baptism of Eros' in *Theology and Sexuality*, vol. 9, no. 2, March 2003, pp. 167–79.

7

Women, Protestantism and the Bible

Meanwhile Mary stayed outside near the tomb, weeping. Then, still weeping, she stooped to look inside, and
saw two angels in white sitting where the body of Jesus
had been, one at the head, the other at the feet. They
said, 'Woman, why are you weeping?' 'They have taken
my Lord away' she replied 'and I don't know where
they have put him.' As she said this she turned round
and saw Jesus standing there, though she did not
recognise him. Jesus said, 'Woman, why are you weeping? Who are you looking for?' Supposing him to be the
gardener, she said, 'Sir, if you have taken him away, tell
me where you have put him, and I will go and remove
him.' Jesus said, 'Mary!' She knew him then and said
to him in Hebrew, 'Rabbuni!' – which means Master.
Jesus said to her, 'Do not cling to me, because I have
not yet ascended to the Father. But go and find the
brothers, and tell them: I am ascending to my Father
and your Father, to my God and your God.' So Mary of
Magdala went and told the disciples that she had seen
the Lord and that he had said these things to her.

(John 20:11–18)

The question of gender and sexual difference takes on different contours if one approaches it from a Protestant
rather than a Catholic perspective. When Protestantism
turned its back on the sacramentality and symbolism of
Catholic Christianity, it also divested the sexual body of its
overtly religious significance. In Protestant churches even
today, sexuality remains largely a question of morals

rather than of symbols. As far as women are concerned, this is a mixed blessing. On the one hand, it has made the struggle for ordination easier in many Protestant churches, because sexual difference has no liturgical significance. Protestant worship has always focused on the preaching of the word rather than the sacramentality of the material world, and the word theoretically transcends the body's materiality, including its sexuality. For most liberal Protestants – including many Anglicans – the sex of the body inside the black ministerial gown or the cassock has no doctrinal significance, once there is an acceptance of the basic social equality of the sexes. For evangelicals who still resist the ordination of women, their arguments tend to be based on biblical passages such as 1 Corinthians 14:34: 'As in all the churches of the saints, women are to remain quiet at meetings since they have no permission to speak; they must keep in the background as the Law itself lays it down.' Such arguments appeal not to the theological sym-bolism of the body, but to its moral significance in the social and sexual hierarchies created by God and revealed in the scriptures.

Moreover, it is significant that the idea of the Mass as a sacrificial cult was vehemently rejected by all the main Reformed churches, and thus the symbolic association between Christian worship and the shedding of blood was done away with. The Protestant communion service is celebrated as a shared meal – sometimes referred to as the Lord's Supper – rather than as participation in a sacrifice. Although since the Second Vatican Council there has been debate in the Roman Catholic Church about the associa-tion of priesthood with sacrifice, it nevertheless remains at least implicitly a significant aspect of the symbolic action of the priest. If we bear in mind the discussion in the last chapter about the religious significance of blood, then it could be argued that women are more likely to be accepted in ministerial roles when those roles are not understood as sacrificial. So in those parts of the Christian tradition such as Roman Catholicism and High Anglicanism, which retain the symbolic significance of sacrifice in their worship, it is not surprising that there is more resistance to women's ordination than in churches which have done away with the idea of sacrifice altogether.

But to what extent does the apparent equality of the sexes in liberal Protestantism and Anglicanism constitute an acceptance of woman *qua* woman? Does the word really transcend the body, or is it more complicated than that? I have already referred to the challenges that women face in finding a language that expresses their difference before God, and to arguments offered by Gilligan and Elshtain that modern society silences women's voices by depriving women's roles and relationships of any significance in the public sphere. Critical theorists and linguists debate the extent to which gender shapes language. Influenced by continental thinkers such as Irigaray, Kristeva and Jacques Lacan, a growing number of feminist theologians are exploring the ways in which theological language is gendered, not only in its explicitly masculine and feminine expressions, but also in its structures and in the values it communicates. From this perspective, it is not enough simply to use inclusive language. Calling God 'she' rather than 'he' means little if all our ideas about God are shaped by traditionally masculine values of power, transcendence and rationality. I was reminded of this in church one Sunday when a priest, in a well-meaning gesture of inclusivity, changed the words of the hymn 'Onward Christian Soldiers' so that he sang 'Sisters we are marching . . .', instead of 'Brothers we are marching . . .'. Such tactics are about as effective in the feminization of Christian worship as the leadership of Margaret Thatcher was in the feminization of British politics.

In worship, we enter most fully into what Heidegger calls 'the house of language'. Every aspect of our daily lives is rendered meaningful by the fact that we are creatures of language who, usually without being conscious that we are doing so, attach coherence and value to events through acts of selective remembering, forgetting and connecting, through naming, describing and communicating. We are constantly telling stories about ourselves, in the words we choose, the inflections we use, the gestures that often unwittingly betray us and invite interpretations other than those we intend. But in worship all this becomes conscious and deliberate. We become performers of ritual, narrative and gesture. We come with others into the presence of a God whom we know that we cannot know or name or approach, and there we are bold to say that we do indeed know and name and approach God by entering into linguistic worlds of imagination, inspiration, revelation and celebration. But where do our bodies belong in this house of language? What meanings do we inscribe on our own flesh in the words that we use, so that when we leave the church we are marked by the texts of prayer and holiness, as bodies that bear religious significance?

Protestantism eliminated the sacramentality of sexual difference from its worship, but it did not thereby transcend sex. Rather, it elevated one sex – the male sex – as the bearer of meaning and the image of God, and transformed the female body into a functional appendage intended only for marriage and procreation. The virginal life was no longer seen as one of value for women, because it denied the purpose for which woman was created by God. Martin Luther quipped, 'Women are created for no other purpose than to serve men and be their helpers. If women grow weary or even die while bearing children, that doesn't harm anything. Let them bear children to death; they are created for that.'[1]

The most violent energies of the reformers were directed towards the destruction of the maternal feminine aspects of the Catholic faith. The Virgin Mary and the saints, including a host of female saints, were purged from worship and devotion, across northern Europe their statues were defaced and vandalized, and shrines and places of pilgrimage that were often particularly significant for women were desecrated. Eamonn Duffy, in his book *The Stripping of the Altars*, notes that many of the monastic sites destroyed by Cromwell in the aftermath of the English Reformation were frequented by pregnant women and women in labour. Duffy comments, 'In attacking monastic "superstition", ... Cromwell's men were striking at institutions with a central place in popular religious practice, perhaps most unexpectedly in the domestic intimacies of pregnancy and childbirth.'[2]

Yet while the symbolic female body was the target of such fury, there was no corresponding attempt to rehabilitate the real female body into Christian language and worship. Indeed, as I have already argued, the place of woman in the Church has been one of the very few constants in the Christian tradition across schisms, reformations and revolutions. So the Reformation created a disembodied and defeminized Christian culture in which the word alone prevailed, and this was often accompanied by a virulent repression of the materiality and spiritual fecundity of human life, particularly as far as women were concerned. It is not coincidental that, although the witch hunts were given their ecclesiastical justification by the publication of *The Malleus Maleficarum* (*The Hammer of the Witches*) in 1486, they reached their murderous climax in the centuries after the Reformation, as the men of church, science and state together waged war on the female body in deed as well as in language and worship.[3]

Lars von Trier's film, *Breaking the Waves*, is a bleak

portrayal of one woman's sexual and spiritual struggle in a small Scottish Presbyterian community. Bess, who represents what Irigaray calls *'la mystérique'*[4] – the mystic who is labelled hysteric by a male-dominated society that cannot understand or accommodate her – breaks free of the repression of her community and experiences a honeymoon period of sexual love for which she gives ecstatic thanks to God. But God, who only towards the end of the film becomes other than a projection of the elders of the kirk, appears to demand endless reparation from Bess for the abundance of her desire, so that in the end her sexuality becomes the source of her martyrdom and her husband's salvation. It is a rich, disturbing and provocative portrayal of feminine holiness, but it sets out in extreme form the plight of the woman as sexual outsider, in the austerely masculine world of Calvinism.

Of course, few Protestant communities are as strict or forbidding as that portrayed by von Trier, but even in liberal churches women still struggle to break free of masculine definitions and norms. Over the years I have worked with a number of women Methodist ministers, and even after thirty years of women's ordination, they still experience a struggle to be women in a church defined and governed by men. In the Church of England, ordination has been a bitter victory for women who find themselves battling against a long tradition of misogyny and a deep suspicion of the woman as priest. One woman describes how a male parishioner spat in her face, because he could not accept her priesthood. Others write of the stress and exhaustion they experience, in struggling to cope not only with hostility to their ministry but also with a system that presumes every vicar has a wife who looks after the children, does the housekeeping, and acts as an unpaid pastoral assistant.[5]

Yet for all these difficulties, women can and do make a difference. I can remember one day walking through the

English countryside, and stopping to visit a small village church. Sometimes these can be depressing places, where nostalgia takes the place of faith and Christianity is held captive by the heritage industry. But this little church seemed different. The noticeboard showed evidence of a widespread concern, not only for the kind of charitable causes that fit comfortably with the *status quo*, but also for issues such as domestic violence and the prison system. It was a place where tradition and change, society and spirituality, had been integrated into something that spoke of life and vision beyond the immediate interests of a small and privileged community. Then I saw the name of the vicar, and it was a woman. Without wanting to oversimplify issues, that seemed partly to explain the difference. In a subtle but important way, she had shifted the image of the Church by what she put on the noticeboard. She had changed the language and the symbols, and in so doing she had invited people to change their way of viewing the world.

For women in the Protestant churches then, the theological task might mean resisting the androgyny of a desexualized and de-eroticized language of worship, in order to redeem the symbolics and sacramentality of sexual difference. The resources for this task lie partly in reclaiming those aspects of the Catholic tradition that offer an authentic and life-giving vision of maternal femininity, but it also might mean recognizing the many ways in which Protestant women no less than Catholic women have contributed to the shaping of theology and worship. That contribution remains masked and therefore it is not easily recognized as a potential site of sexual difference where women might find symbols and images of faith other than those to be found in the dominant masculine tradition. One example recently identified by Valentine Cunningham is the fact that so many of the great Victorian hymns were written by women, and that the language and imagery does

indeed suggest 'a different voice': 'Into a religious world
managed by men, these women subversively interposed
words, feelings, experiences manifestly from the female
sphere. This was the subaltern majority in the pew taking
over, as it were, the pulpits from which they were excluded.'
He points to the recurring images of motherhood, self-sur-
render, erotic abandonment and blood that all suggest a
profound identification with Christ: 'When these writers
think about the blood of Christ it's with a complicity the
male hymn-writers can never share. For these poets bleed
too, because they menstruate – which makes them taboo
and in their own way outsiders, like the dying Jesus.'[6] The
women's historian, Susan Morgan, argues that evangelicalism
gave Victorian women a platform from which to campaign
and influence the public sphere in significant ways, despite
their apparent exclusion from positions of authority.[7]
Women such as Josephine Butler, who campaigned vigorously on behalf of prostitutes, were inspired by their faith to
defy the social restrictions and taboos of their society.
Florence Nightingale, benignly remembered for her brief
role in the Crimea as the Lady of the Lamp, was in fact a
woman who might have been more at home in the company
of Wollstonecraft than her middle-class Victorian contemporaries. Valerie Webb's recent study of Nightingale
describes her as 'a radical theologian' who once said, 'When
very many years ago I planned a future, my one idea was
not organizing a hospital but organizing a religion.'[8] Webb
writes, 'The more I read Florence's immense literary
output, the more I encountered a "God-intoxicated being"
whose reform was not her goal in life but the *consequence*
of her religion. Florence cannot be interpreted outside the
parameter of a woman in love with, and loved by, God and
absorbed with deepening that relationship.'[9]

     This retrieval of the spiritual dimension of women's
lives faces two challenges. On the one hand, there is the

ongoing struggle to authenticate these theological visions
so that they become a recognized part of the Christian
heritage, not by being subsumed into an existing language
and culture, but by opening up the spiritual imagination to
voices of difference. But there is also the need to resist a
secular feminist endeavour that, in the process of retrieving
women's histories, tends to eradicate the 'god-intoxicated'
dimension of their lives. This has the effect of negating the
positive role played by faith in women's historical struggles for a sense of meaning and selfhood, so that feminist
history in the end records only the destructive and negative aspects of faith, and denies women access to any
dimension of the Christian understanding of God in their
quest for meaning.

As with all other aspects of history, the Reformation and
its aftermath cannot be reduced to simply one narrative with
regard to its impact on women's lives. While it led to the
impoverishment of symbols, values and religious ideas associated with motherhood in particular, it also provided opportunities and possibilities for women in the Church. New
religious movements tend to be less rigid in their gender
roles and hierarchies than those with established structures
and institutions, and the Reformation was no exception, with
groups such as the Quakers, the Anabaptists and the Pietists
affording women new spaces of spiritual authority and
freedom.[10] Bonnie Anderson and Judith Zinsser write that
'for women, whether Protestant or Catholic, the roles opened
to them in the early centuries of Christianity opened to them
again in the spiritual chaos and competition for souls in the
sixteenth and seventeenth centuries. ... For the second time
in history, religious faith gave Christian women access to
authority within their churches and the opportunity to act as
the spiritual and actual equals of men.'[11]

Sometimes, women's battles for recognition and equality in the period after the Reformation were conducted in

heated debate with their clerical counterparts, as with the English pamphleteers who were active in the late sixteenth century. Women such as Jane Anger engaged in energetic polemics against those who sought to revive the misogynist arguments of medieval and patristic theology. It will give a sense of the rhetorical flourish of these debates to quote from one of Anger's pamphlets:

> The creation of man and woman at the first, he being formed *In principio* of dross and filthy clay, did so remain until God saw that in him his workmanship was good, and therefore by the transformation of the dust which was loathsome unto flesh it became purified. Then lacking a help for him, God, making woman of man's flesh that she might be purer than he, doth evidently show how far we women are more excellent than men. Our bodies are fruitful, whereby the world increaseth, and our care wonderful, by which man is preserved. From woman sprang man's salvation. A woman was the first that believed, and a woman likewise the first that repented of sin.[12]

Anger's appeal to the Genesis story is a reminder that, if men have used the authority of the Bible to justify the subordination of women, women have also turned to the Bible to challenge that interpretation. The feminist historian, Gerda Lerner, describes how her research led her to recognize the positive influence of religion in women's struggles for freedom. She writes, 'The insight that religion was the primary arena on which women fought for hundreds of years for feminist consciousness was not one I had previously had.'[13] In her two volume study of western women's history, Lerner includes a chapter called 'One Thousand Years of Feminist Bible Criticism'. She writes:

Since male objections to women thinking, teaching and speaking in public were for centuries based on biblical authority, the development of feminist Bible criticism can be seen as an appropriate and perhaps not unexpected response to the constraints and limitations imposed upon women's intellectual development by religiously sanctioned gender definitions. These biblical core texts sat like huge boulders across the paths women had to travel in order to define themselves as equals of men.[14]

There is much work still to be done in retrieving and collating women's theological and biblical writings through the centuries, but today feminist biblical studies is a growing field of scholarship, and it remains one of the most significant areas for developing the unexplored possibilities of the Christian story from the perspective of women. Feminist biblical hermeneutics involves interpreting the Bible in relation to particular contexts and questions related to women, rather than assuming the position of the neutral and detached interpreter. Of course, Protestants have always read the Bible in a personal, subjective context, seeking guidance, wisdom and inspiration – a practice that only in the latter half of the twentieth century was encouraged among ordinary Catholics. But this kind of devotional reading is different from interpretative practices in which one deliberately positions oneself in the context of a community or group that has been socially marginalized for reasons of sex, race or class, to ask what new revelations come into view from this changed perspective. This form of interpretation originated with Catholic liberation theology, which sought to read the Bible in political and social engagement with the struggles of the poor, but it has become widespread practice by many feminist and liberationist interpreters from different cultures and traditions.

It has particular relevance for women in churches that place a high premium on the authority of the Bible, because it is through opening up a plurality of meanings and interpretations that it becomes possible to challenge the one-sided and often authoritarian rules that are justified through an appeal to Scripture, particularly in matters of gender and sexuality.

In assuming interpretative positions where partiality and bias are acknowledged rather than denied, feminists and others would argue that they are simply exposing what has always been the case. Any text, including the Bible, is read in its cultural and social contexts, and therefore it has imposed upon it the hidden dynamics of power and meaning through which social and sexual hierarchies are sustained. This is particularly true when that text has the authority and status of the Bible. In religious communities, those who control scriptural meanings acquire significant power over society. The martyrdom of figures such as William Tyndale shows the extent to which the democratization of scripture poses a threat to those whose power is sustained by the authority to read and interpret. If the invention of the printing press signalled the beginning of the end of clerical power in Europe, the growing number of women theologians and biblical scholars might no less signal the end of male power in the Church.

The Bible was written by men in patriarchal societies, and from a feminist perspective many biblical passages remain problematic even when they are divested of their layers of historical interpretation. However, feminist scholars are also demonstrating the extent to which the Bible is a multifaceted collection of writings that has been made to conform too easily to the dictates and values of patriarchy. Its ambiguities and apparent contradictions sometimes militate against human equality and freedom, but its central theme is that of a God who has a special concern for the

little people, the *anawim*, of history. So, for example, while
the Old Testament reflects the patriarchal values of the
societies in which it was written, it includes stories of
women such as Ruth and Naomi, Sarah and Hagar,
Deborah, Abigail, Esther and Hannah, all of whom in various ways subvert male authority and become figures chosen
by God as particular sources of revelation. While the God of
the Old Testament is masculine, he is frequently invested
with feminine qualities (see the next chapter). The presence
of God, the *shekinah* in Hebrew, is a feminine bridal presence that comes to dwell among the people in the Sabbath
celebration, and the wisdom of God, *sophia* in Greek,
hokmah in Hebrew, is always depicted as feminine. Some see
in these feminized aspects of God a suggestion of the divine
consort of the pagan religions, who was repressed but not
entirely eliminated from the religion of the Jewish people.

In the New Testament, the Gospels provide no ammu-
nition for those who would marginalize women in the
Church. Women play a central role as disciples in the
ministry of Jesus, often at crucial moments of decision or
revelation. For example, one of the main arguments used
by the Catholic hierarchy for the exclusion of women
from the sacramental priesthood is that Jesus chose only
men to be his apostles. But all four Gospels refer to
women as being the first witnesses to the resurrection,
and in John's Gospel this includes Jesus sending Mary
Magdalene to be the first one to tell the disciples the good
news. In the early and medieval Church, Mary Magdalene
was known as the apostle to the apostles. Today, one
might argue that she is in fact the first preacher commis-
sioned by Christ, as a potent sign that in the post-
resurrection world of the Church, Jesus chooses women
to be the first among equals. This is particularly
significant if one bears in mind that women's witness had
no legal status in the Jewish world.

As more and more feminist scholars study and interpret
the Bible, we must expect its women characters to come
more clearly into the picture. Although the Pauline epistles
– written before the Gospels – already show signs of a
gendered power struggle in the early Church, with men
seeking to assert their authority over women, there are
also many references to women who were active in roles of
ministry and leadership. Women such as Phoebe (Rom.
16:1), Priscilla (Rom. 16:3), and Eudia and Syntyche (Phil.
4:2) are among those mentioned by name. Another, Junia
(Rom. 16:7), was renamed Junias – a man's name – at some
stage in the transmission of the text, perhaps because the
transcriber could not understand a woman being referred
to as one of the 'outstanding apostles'.

The task of feminist biblical criticism is both historical
and exegetical. Some scholars such as Elisabeth Schüssler
Fiorenza read the scriptures in their historical and social
contexts, in order to reconstruct the lives of women in the
early Church. Fiorenza has played a key role in retrieving
the stories of the women leaders and deacons of the New
Testament and post-apostolic Church, suggesting a
Christian movement that was radically egalitarian and
counter-cultural in its early days, but that gradually
became organized around more rigid gendered hierarchies
as its institutions and structures took shape.[15] Other scholars such as Trible, whose work I have already mentioned,
focus on literary analysis of the scriptural texts to show
that they are invested with subtle and complex meanings
that often destabilize rather than affirm gender hierarchies and traditional readings. In particular, Trible offers a
rich and nuanced re-reading of the story of creation and
the fall in Genesis, to show that it is an unfolding tragedy,
'a love story gone awry'[16] in which the initial *eros* of creation
experienced as 'unity, fulfillment, harmony and delight',[17]
yields to death or *thanatos*, as a result of which 'imperfec-

tions become problems, distinctions become oppositions, hierarchies become oppressions, and joy dissipates into unrelieved tragedy. Life loses to Death.'[18] Elsewhere, she offers a powerful feminist reclamation of the story of the unnamed woman in Judges 19:1–30, a concubine whose master hands her over to a hostile crowd of men to be raped and murdered. In Trible's reading, the woman's murder stands as a judgement on those who killed her, and her dismemberment has eucharistic associations. Finally, she quotes from the scriptural account: 'Direct your heart to her, take counsel, and speak' (Judg. 20:7). She writes,

> Truly, to speak for this woman is to interpret against the narrator, plot, other characters, and the biblical tradition because they have shown her neither compassion nor attention. . . . Misogyny belongs to every age, including our own. Violence and vengeance are not just characteristics of a distant, pre-Christian past; they infect the community of the elect to this day. Woman as object is still captured, betrayed, raped, tortured, murdered, dismembered, and scattered. To take to heart this ancient story, then, is to confess its present reality. The story is alive, and all is not well. Beyond confession we must take counsel to say, 'Never again.' Yet this counsel is itself ineffectual unless we direct our hearts to that most uncompromising of all biblical commands, speaking the word not to others but to ourselves: Repent. Repent.[19]

Thus from the perspective of feminist biblical scholarship, one of the most apparently misogynist and violent of all the biblical texts about women is retrieved and transformed into an elegy for every woman who has suffered abuse because of the tradition of contempt for the female body that I described in the last chapter.

Some of the most interesting and challenging feminist reinterpretations of the Bible come from women of colour and Third World women who bring new questions to bear on readings that have been largely unchallenged in the context of white western Christianity. Many women's theologies have flourished in engagement with feminism, but not necessarily in sympathy with all the arguments of white western feminists. In the quest to express both a relationship to and a distance from western feminism, these diverse theologies use a variety of names to describe themselves. They include, among others, womanist theology (arising out of the experiences of Black North American women), *dalit* women's theology (which explores the situation of low caste Christian women in India), concerned African women's theology (primarily focusing on the encounter between African culture, Christianity and feminism), *minjung* feminist theology (Korean women's theology from the perspective of the poor and the marginalized), and *mujerista* theology (informed by the experiences of Hispanic American women).[20] To give an example of the ways in which these different cultural perspectives inform feminist biblical interpretation, I want to focus on the story of Hagar, Sarah, Ishmael, Isaac and Abraham in Genesis 16:1–14 and 21:9–19.

In the Genesis text, Sarah is infertile so she sends Abraham to conceive a child with her servant, Hagar. But Sarah is consumed by jealousy over Hagar and her son, Ishmael, and when Sarah gives birth to Isaac, she tells Abraham to send Hagar and Ishmael into the wilderness. Sarah, Abraham and Isaac have been key figures throughout Christian history. In Galatians 4:21 – 5:1, Paul contrasts children born of the free woman, Sarah, with children of the slave woman, Hagar, seeing the former as the Church and the latter as the old Jerusalem. Thus from the earliest days, Christians have interpreted this story as one of privilege related to Sarah, and exclusion related to Hagar, in a way that is heavily invested with anti-Jewish polemic. But womanist theologians such as Delores Williams see in Hagar a symbol of sisterhood for Black Christian women who have a history of slavery and oppression by white women as well as by men. Hagar is an Egyptian slave who is abused by her owners and cast out into the desert to fend for herself and her child. But God cares for Hagar and Ishmael, and moreover, Hagar is the only person in the Old Testament to whom is attributed the power of naming God when she says, 'You are El Roi' (Gen. 16:13). Williams writes, 'Hagar, like many black women, goes into the wide world to make a living for herself and her child, with only God by her side.'[21]

Mukti Barton, an Indian theologian, offers a different interpretation of Hagar and Sarah in her study of women in Bangladesh, where most of the population is Muslim. Muslims trace their religious genealogy through Hagar, Abraham and Ishmael rather than through Sarah, Abraham and Isaac, so the story provides a point of encounter between Muslims and Christians. But in the present global economy, Barton also identifies Sarah with white western feminists, and Hagar with poor Bangladeshi women. She writes,

If the narrative of Hagar is compared to the current international power struggle, a Bangladeshi woman can be seen as Hagar and her Euro-American sister as Sarah. A Bangladeshi woman can easily be identified as the gentile slave, because she too is dispossessed on account of her ethnicity and economic and political standing as well as her gender. Nationally and inter-nationally a Bangladeshi woman is the exploited one. Sarah is also under the constriction of patriarchy, but she is not dispossessed in every sense. ... Just as the biblical Hagar could gain nothing by identifying with Sarah as long as Sarah remained the oppressor, so Bangladeshi women cannot possibly benefit from connecting with western feminists until racial, economic and political divisions are acknowledged as clearly as gender issues in their feminism.[22]

While womanist and Bangladeshi representations of Hagar are motivated by the same sense of identification with a woman who finds herself the victim of patriarchy because of her gender, her ethnicity and her social status, their different theological contexts give rise to different interpretations and emphases.

Womanist writings offer a dynamic feminist reappropriation of a Protestantism that has been the vehicle of both slavery and emancipation for black Americans. Novelists and poets such as Toni Morrison, Audre Lorde and Alice Walker create spiritual visions of struggle, courage and sexual self-expression that weave Christian themes and images into new configurations, while exposing the extent to which Christianity has been complicit in America's history of slavery, racism and misogyny. Theologians such as Delores Williams, Katie G. Cannon and Jacquelyn Grant revisit the texts of the Bible and theology to raise questions and propose meanings that sometimes seem to challenge the foundations of Christian doctrine and ethics. Williams, for example, asks to what extent the doctrine of the atonement – the belief that Christ suffered and died for us – advocates a form of surrogate suffering that tended to endorse rather than challenge the exploitation and abuse of black women by their white masters and mistresses. She suggests that images of Christ as the surrogate victim who suffers and dies on behalf of others are deeply problematic for black American women, whose history of slavery, servitude and sexual abuse has too often made them suffering surrogates for others. [23]

Cannon calls into question the whole tradition of
Christian ethics and its relevance for Black American communities. Recalling her quest to find a set of values that
were relevant to people in the Black churches, she writes,

> When I turned specifically to theological ethics, I dis-
> covered the dominant ethical systems implied that the
> doing of Christian ethics in the Black community was
> either immoral or amoral. The cherished ethical ideas
> predicated upon the existence of freedom and a wide
> range of choices proved null and void in situations of
> oppression. The real-lived texture of Black life
> requires moral agency that may run contrary to the
> ethical boundaries of mainline Protestantism. Blacks
> may use action guides that have never been consid-
> ered within the scope of traditional codes of faithful
> living. Racism, gender discrimination and economic
> exploitation, as inherited, age-long complexes, require
> the Black community to create and cultivate values
> and virtues in their own terms so that they prevail
> against the odds with moral integrity.[24]

Cannon proposes the Black women's literary tradition as
an alternative resource for the construction of ethics,
weaving together as it does the forgotten stories, folk tales
and oral traditions of Black people's histories.

These multicultural theological visions pose some of the
most radical challenges to western Christianity, as they
refigure the insights and arguments of feminist theology
from the perspectives of those who have suffered multiple
forms of social and symbolic exclusion on account of gender, race, culture and class. To recognize this is not to deny
the long process that lies ahead, of consolidating these
many different visions into a coherent Christian narrative
that will be enlarged and enriched in ways that we cannot

yet imagine by the participation of so many excluded voices. It remains to be seen how flexible Christian doctrine must be, and how far indeed the boundaries of the Christian faith might stretch before they dissolve into an impossible plurality of beliefs and convictions. But around the world there is today a multitude of women from every creed, denomination and culture, looking anew to the promises of the Christian story and asking what riches it might yield if it is liberated from its captivity to a western androcentric vision of God and the world.

An underlying issue in this ongoing process of Christian feminist scholarship is that of the relationship between revelation, history and culture in the writing and interpretation of the scriptures. Only the most fundamentalist Christians today would deny that the Bible is the work of many authors and that its message is influenced by the contexts in which it was written. Although there is still much debate about the authorship and dating of the New Testament texts, it is widely accepted that the Pauline epistles predate the Gospels, and that the latter probably represent four different ways of representing the life of Christ as it was preserved in the oral traditions of the very early Church. From the late nineteenth century, a secular, scientific approach to knowledge became the norm in western scholarship, including Protestant biblical studies. Setting aside questions of revelation and truth, biblical scholars focused instead on the historical and literary meanings of the texts. Although this initially met with resistance from the Catholic Church, during the twentieth century it gradually gained acceptance so that from the 1950s Catholic biblical scholars have had a notable influence on the field. However, recent years have seen the re-emergence of a more narrative approach to the Bible, so that it is read primarily not as an historical document but as part of the Church's story.[25] From this perspective, there is a recognition that the authors of the Gospels were not setting out to give an historical account of Jesus' life and times, but to narrate his story retrospectively, in the light of the Resurrection and the faith of the early Church. More controversially perhaps, this approach brings with it the claim that the Christian faith community, not the secular academy, has the authority to interpret and explore the scriptures. To say this is not to reject academic scholarship, but it is to reject the claims to objectivity, historicity and critical distance that are the hallmarks of modern secular studies. Postmodernism, with its acknowledgement of subjectivity, partiality and the complex interaction between texts, authors and readers, legitimates such shifts in the intellectual climate of contemporary Christian scholarship, but it brings both risks and opportunities for feminist scholars.

On the one hand, a postmodernist approach creates a relatively open space of engagement between women readers and the biblical texts. We are not bound by past readings nor by authoritative intepretations, but can enter into a dynamic exchange where our lives become caught up anew in the possibilities and challenges of the narrative. Thus the rigid meanings of the past dissolve and become suffused with poetry and promise, and also with fury and despair, as reading becomes an act of exposure, struggle, discovery and challenge. But it also runs the risk of capitulating to a form of relativism in which readings and interpretations proliferate with no sense of an authoritative framework within which some interpretations are recognized as more legitimate than others. Does this matter? My own suggestion is that the Bible itself forms the focal point – the prism – through which these many different perspectives are refracted. In this way, one might imagine the white light of revelation passing through the biblical narratives in such a way that these become a shared world

of symbols, meanings and referents for interpreting the
human condition in all its historical and cultural contexts,
giving rise to a rainbow-coloured multitude of different
ways of living and expressing the Christian faith.

But I also think that the ongoing conversation between
tradition and scripture is important for women, and to
explain why I want to return to the figure of Mary
Magdalene. In recent years, a number of books have been
written that analyse the biblical and historical figure of
Mary Magdalene. In the Catholic tradition, she has traditionally been depicted as a penitent prostitute, despite the
fact that she is never described in that way in the Bible.
Scholars such as Esther de Boer and Carla Ricci argue per-
suasively that the traditional association of Mary
Magdalene with the penitent sexual sinner obscures her
role as one of the most significant women disciples,
and once again sets up associations between the female
body and fallen sexuality that are detrimental to the rep-
resentation of women.[26] However, I want to suggest an
alternative possibility that might reconcile these two quite
different images of the same woman.

Of all the images of women in the Catholic tradition,
that of Mary Magdalene is one of the most complex and
interesting. She is usually identifiable by the symbol of a
jar that associates her with the woman who anointed
Jesus, although the Bible does not actually identify her as
such. Paintings of the Resurrection often depict her in the
garden with Jesus. Titian's *'Noli me tangere'* ('Do not
touch me'), in the National Gallery, shows Christ in a complex gesture of desire and evasion, twisting his groin away
from her outstretched hand. It is interesting to compare
this with another work in the National Gallery by
Bernardo Strozzi, titled 'The Incredulity of Saint Thomas',
which shows Thomas putting his fingers in the risen
Christ's wounds in an act with implicitly sexual overtones.

But the most common image of Mary Magdalene is that of her standing beside the mother of Jesus at the foot of the cross, or caressing the feet of the dead Christ as he is taken down from the cross, watched over by the grieving figure of the Virgin Mary. These images are inspired by the mistaken association of Mary Magdalene with the woman who anointed the feet of Jesus in Luke's Gospel, but they are suffused with a sense of tenderness and physical potency that does not condemn the sexual female body but elevates it to a position of great intimacy with Christ. I find something powerful and positive about these paintings, where female sexuality and virginity are reconciled and redeemed side by side at the foot of the cross. If Titian's Mary is not allowed to touch the body of the risen Christ, no such taboo prevails in these voluptuous images of loss and longing in which she caresses the crucified body of Christ like a sorrowing lover.

All the alternative metaphors and images that women seek can be retrieved and reinterpreted from such art. This is a woman who expresses herself in touch and gesture, whose sexuality is often highlighted by her scarlet dress and flowing hair, but she stands beside the Virgin Mother in a way that can be seen as reconciling the different dimensions of female sexuality – the virgin, the mother, and the woman whose sexual body has been redeemed by Christ. It is not improbable that in at least some of these images Mary Magdalene is intended to symbolize Eve, the sexual temptress brought into the community of the faithful through the blood of Christ.

But the traditional image of Mary Magdalene is also a reminder that women need sexual healing. Feminist celebrations of female sexuality often fail to acknowledge the sometimes dark and muddled complexity of what it means to be a sexual being, for women as well as for men. While it is true that women's capacity for sexual self-expression has been diminished and repressed by men's fear of the female body in the Christian tradition, post-Christian society has given rise to a burgeoning sex industry in which the combined forces of global communications and widespread poverty have created a subculture of sexual exploitation, abuse and violence against women and children worldwide on an unprecedented scale. I have worked with an ecumenical outreach project with women in prostitution in recent years, and it is impossible to overestimate the destruction that a woman experiences when she sells her body to men on the streets every night. These are women whose souls are ravaged, whose sense of self-worth has been eliminated sometimes through a history of abuse stretching back to early childhood, and who in the last cruel twist often have their children taken away from them because they are incapable of mothering them properly. I cannot describe the grief of one young woman whose toddler had just been taken into care, despite all her efforts to prove that she could look after this small person who was the only source of love and affirmation she had ever had. Such women are gathered into the love of Christ in the person of Mary Magdalene, and that is why I am reluctant to see her tidied up and made respectable. The forgiven and redeemed prostitute turned apostle might be an imaginative construct of the Catholic tradition with little firm basis in scripture, but her presence is a reminder that the sexual female body is brought to wholeness, beauty and grace in Christ, in a way that affirms rather than denies her sexuality. Just look at Masaccio's image of Mary Magdalene at the crucifixion. Her golden hair tumbles down her scarlet cloak, and she throws her arms up in a gesture of abandonment at the feet of the crucified Christ, in an image that does indeed suggest a different voice, a different body, a different way of being before God.

With that in mind, I want to turn at last to the question of God and woman. Who is God for woman, and who is woman for God? Rather than answering this shared mystery of being, I want to suggest that it is in its mystery and unknowability that the question of woman must remain, as an open-ended space of becoming divine in Christ. So I situate the next chapters in the context of sacramentality, prayer and belonging, as the nexus within which I believe the female body might find a space of becoming as the beloved of God.

1 Martin Luther, *D. Martin Luther's sämmtiliche Werke* (Erlangen and Frankfurt, 1826–57), 61, 125, quoted in Merry Wiesner, 'Luther and Women: The Death of Two Marys' in Ann Loades (ed.), *Feminist Theology: A Reader* (London: SPCK, 1990), p. 123.

2 Eamon Duffy, *The Stripping of the Altars: Traditional Religion in England 1400–1580* (New Haven and London: Yale University Press, 1992), p. 385.

3 See Beattie, *Eve's Pilgrimage*, pp. 124–7.

4 See Luce Irigaray, *Speculum of the Other Woman*, trans. Gillian C. Gill (Ithaca, NY: Cornell University Press, 1985), p. 191.

5 See Helen Thorne, *Journey to Priesthood: An In-Depth Study of the First Women Priests in the Church of England*, CCSRG Monograph Series (Bristol: University of Bristol, 2000).

6 Valentine Cunningham, 'The Hymns were Hers: How Victorian Women gave the Anglican Church its Greatest Hits' in The *Guardian*, 30 March 2002 on http://www.guardian.co.uk/Archive/Article/0,4273,4384314,00.html; accessed on 9 April 2002.

7 See Susan Morgan, 'Rethinking History in Gender History: Historiographical and Methodological Reflections' in Ursula King and Tina Beattie (eds.), *Gender, Religion and Diversity: Cross-Cultural Approaches* (London and New York: Continuum, forthcoming).

8 Florence Nightingale, quoted on the back cover of Val Webb, *Florence Nightingale: The Making of a Radical Theologian* (St. Louis, MO: Chalice Press, 2002).

9 Ibid., p. xv.

10 See Gerda Lerner, *The Creation of Feminist Consciousness: From the Middle Ages to Eighteen-seventy* (New York and Oxford: Oxford University Press, 1994), pp. 93–105.

11 Bonnie S. Anderson and Judith P. Zinsser, *A History of Their Own: Women in Europe from Prehistory to the Present*, Vol. 1 (Harmondsworth: Penguin Books, 1988), p. 229.

12 Jane Anger quoted in Lerner, *The Creation of Feminist Consciousness*, p. 151.

13 Ibid., p vii.

14 Ibid., p. 138.

15 See Elisabeth Schüssler Fiorenza, *But She Said – Feminist Practices of Biblical Interpretation* (Boston: Beacon Press, 1992). See also the two volume collection, *Searching the Scriptures*, ed. Fiorenza, 2 vols. (London: SCM Press, 1994 and 1995).

16 Trible, *God and the Rhetoric of Sexuality*, p. 72.

17 Ibid., p. 74.

18 Ibid., p. 74.

19 Phyllis Trible, *Texts of Terror: Literary-Feminist Readings of Biblical Narratives* (Philadelphia: Fortress Press, 1984), pp. 86–7.

20 For examples of these and other women's theologies, see Ursula King (ed.), *Feminist Theology from the Third World: A Reader* (London: SPCK; Maryknoll, NY: Orbis Press, 1994).

21 Delores S. Williams, *Sisters in the Wilderness. The Challenge of Womanist God-Talk* (Maryknoll, NY: Orbis Press, 1993), p. 33.

22 Mukti Barton, *Scripture as Empowerment for Liberation and Justice. The Experience of Christian and Muslim Women in Bangladesh*, CCSRG Monograph Series (Bristol: University of Bristol, 1999), p. 137.

23 See Delores S. Williams, 'Black Women's Surrogacy Experience' in Paula M. Cooey, William R. Eakin and Jay B. McDaniel (eds.), *After Patriarchy: Feminist Transformations of the World Religions* (Maryknoll, NY: Orbis Books, 1993).

24 Katie Geneva Cannon, 'Moral Wisdom in the Black Women's Literary Tradition' in Judith Plaskow and Carol P. Christ (eds.) *Weaving the Visions: New Patterns in Feminist Spirituality* (San Francisco: HarperSanFrancisco, 1989), p. 282.

25 See Gerard Loughlin, *Telling God's Story* (Cambridge: Cambridge University Press, 1996).

26 See Carla Ricci, *Mary Magdalene and Many Others: Women who followed Jesus,* trans. Paul Burns (Tunbridge Wells: Burns & Oates, 1994); Esther de Boer, *Mary Magdalene: Beyond the Myth*, trans. John Bowden (London: SCM Press, 1997).

8

Woman, Sacramentality and the Image of God

For by the light of understanding within your light I have tasted and seen your depth, eternal Trinity, and the beauty of your creation. Then, when I considered myself in you, I saw that I am your image. You have gifted me with power from yourself, eternal Father, and my understanding with your wisdom – such wisdom as is proper to your only-begotten Son; and the Holy Spirit, who proceeds from you and from your Son, has given me a will, and so I am able to love.

You, eternal Trinity, are the craftsman; and I your handiwork have come to know that you are in love with the beauty of what you have made, since you made of me a new creation in the blood of your Son.

Catherine of Siena, 1347–80[1]

Feminist theologians argue that Christian theological language has become trapped in a patriarchal and androcentric mindset that prevents us from appreciating the many possibilities for speaking about God in terms of different relationships, metaphors and symbols. While, on the one hand, all Christian theologians would agree that God cannot be defined in language and that the divine is ultimately beyond gender, there is still deep resistance in the modern Church to speaking of God in anything other than the language of fatherhood and masculinity.

The idea of God as a father figure modelled along the lines of patriarchal authority came to prominence in

Christian theology after the conversion of Rome, when the social and sexual hierarchies of the ancient world began to pervade Christian ideas and institutions in a more thorough way than before. Jürgen Moltmann argues that the 'Romanisation of the image of God … involved transferring the Roman *patria potestas* to God',[2] so that after the fourth century God becomes identified with a more domineering and authoritarian image of fatherhood. Elshtain suggests that this was given added impetus after the Reformation, when Protestantism banished the maternal feminine aspects of the medieval Church and 'A more stern and forbidding image of the patriarchal God emerged.'[3]

However, notwithstanding such arguments, the language of fatherhood pervades the texts and traditions of Christianity, so that either one has to argue, with post-Christian feminists such as Mary Daly and Daphne Hampson, that the Christian faith is irredeemably patriarchal and therefore oppressive for women at least by contemporary social standards, or one has to reassess the value of paternal language in order to bring to the fore its positive potential for signifying relationships of fatherly tenderness and love. Otherwise, there is a risk of simply reversing and therefore reinforcing dualistic stereotypes, by substituting matriarchal and maternal imagery for patriarchal and paternal imagery, in a way that fails to challenge the association of fatherhood with authoritarianism and tyranny. Not only does this evacuate much of the language of the Christian tradition of any positive value or meaning, it is also an ethical violation against the importance of fatherhood in domestic and social life, as a role that can be – and indeed should be – a sharing of the vocation to raise children in an atmosphere of love, nurture and mutual endeavour. By understanding the fatherhood of God in terms of qualities of tenderness, solicitude and compassion more commonly associated with maternal stereotypes, it becomes a judgement against men who use the paternal role to justify the abuse of power and to transform domestic life into mini-dictatorships of tyranny and fear.

The idea of God as a loving father is one that belongs particularly to Christianity, and that comes into focus in the Gospels. In bringing the fatherhood of God to the foreground of prayer and devotion, Christ invited his followers as brothers and sisters into a relationship with God modelled on his own. We are all to become children of God, not as a distant authority figure but as a tender and intimate father who numbers the very hairs on our heads. Paul Ricoeur argues that the biblical story represents a rejection of the oedipal father gods of the pagan cults in the Old Testament, and inaugurates a new, non-oedipal form of divine fatherhood in Christ's teachings in the New Testament.[4] By bringing into play a variety of metaphors for the relationship between God and humankind, the cult of divine fatherhood can be relativized while retaining its capacity to communicate the deeply personal exchange of love and intimacy that is epitomized in the relationship between Christ the Son and God the Father.

The Old Testament has relatively few references to God as father, with a more common image being of God as the husband of Israel. But this is still only one of an abundance of metaphors drawn from human relationships and from the natural world to express Israel's experience of God. The book of the prophet Hosea, for example, is an intricate weaving together of paternal and nuptial imagery to suggest the faithful love of God for Israel, which is depicted as both an adulterous wife and a defiant son. There are a number of places where the Old Testament writers use maternal imagery for God, as in Isaiah 49:15, where God's love for Israel is compared to a mother's love for her child: 'Can a mother forget the baby at her breast and have no compassion on the child she has borne? Though she may

forget, I will not forget you!' God's challenge to Job is one
of the most richly metaphorical chapters of the Bible, and it
invokes a plurality of images to describe the creative activity of God, including both maternal and paternal images:

> Does the rain have a father?
> Who fathers the drops of dew?
> From whose womb comes the ice?
> Who gives birth to the frost from the heavens
> when the waters become hard as stone,
> when the surface of the deep is frozen?
> (Job 38:28–30).

In Isaiah there is a startling juxtaposition of masculine
and feminine imagery in two verses that read as follows:

> The Lord will march out like a mighty man,
> like a warrior he will stir up his zeal;
> with a shout he will raise the battle cry
> and will triumph over his enemies.

> 'For a long time I have kept silent,
> I have been quiet and held myself back.
> But now, like a woman in childbirth,
> I cry out, I gasp and pant.'
> (Is. 42:13–14).

Of particular interest in this text is that, while the
prophet represents God as an avenging warrior in the third
person, when God speaks in the first person it is in the language of a mother bringing her child to birth.

In the New Testament Jesus likens himself to a mother
hen protecting her young: 'O Jerusalem, Jerusalem, you
who kill the prophets and stone those sent to you, how
often I have longed to gather your children together, as a

hen gathers her chicks under her wings, but you were not willing!' (Lk. 13:34). For Christian thinkers such as St Anselm, writing in the twelfth century, such biblical metaphors inspired reflection on the maternal qualities of Christ. Anselm writes:

> And you, my soul, dead in yourself,
> run under the wings of Jesus your mother
> and lament your griefs under his feathers. . . .
>
> Christ, my mother,
> you gather your chickens under your wings;
> this dead chicken of yours puts himself under those wings.[5]

Anselm's prayer is a reminder that, in the Middle Ages, gendered symbolism was used to express the many different qualities and attributes of God. Motherhood and fatherhood were not understood only in terms of biological functions but in terms of social roles and relationships. Mystics such as Hildegard of Bingen and Julian of Norwich were able to draw on a range of maternal and feminine metaphors when seeking to express the creativity and love of God. For Julian, the idea of motherhood can only be fully understood in the context of God's creative love:

> This fair, lovely word 'mother' is so sweet and so natural in itself that it cannot truly be said of anyone but Him, or to anyone but Him, Who is the true Mother of life and of everything. To motherhood as properties belong natural love, wisdom and knowledge – and this is God. For though it is true that our bodily bringing forth is very little, low and simple compared to our spiritual bringing forth, yet it is He who does the mothering through the creatures by whom it is done.[6]

Hildegard of Bingen draws on the biblical imagery of
divine wisdom as a feminine aspect of God when she writes
of Wisdom as 'a figure of great beauty' who 'shines in him
as a great adornment, being the broadest step amongst the
steps of the other virtues in him. She is joined to him in a
dance, in the sweetest embrace of blazing love.'[7]

So when feminist theologians today appeal for a greater
appreciation of the potential plurality of theological language, it can be argued that this invites a move away from
the rigidities and literalisms of modern theology, to a more
traditional and holistic way of thinking about God. In addition, the Christian doctrine of the Trinity – the belief that
God is three persons in one – must be allowed to situate all
theological reflection in a space of profound mystery, so
that every theory, argument or claim about God, however
persuasive or truthful it might appear to be, unravels on
the central and inscrutable mystery of the Trinity.
Catherine Mowry LaCugna looks to Trinitarian theology
for a model of interpersonal relationships of loving equality
in difference, in which humankind is invited to share in
the divine life, in a way that has radical implications for
our understanding of salvation, history and society.[8]
Through our intimate communion with the Trinitarian
God, we are drawn into relationships of mutual giving and
receiving of self, which constitute the meaning of personhood and the inner life of the Trinity.

With the foregoing in mind, I want to reflect on the
theology of the fourteenth century saint and mystic,
Catherine of Siena, in order to suggest that, while she
presents a number of problems for modern interpreters,
Catherine's writings open a doorway into the complexity
and promise of the Christian understanding of God for
women today, even allowing for the vast cultural and
historical differences between us. Through a creative
appropriation of the style, imagery and ethics of

Catherine's theology, I believe it is possible to reclaim an alternative way of speaking with and about God that remains faithful to the Christian tradition while allowing for a deepened appreciation of the significance of language, sacramentality and embodiment for Christian female personhood.

Sacramentality refers to the Christian belief that the material world is suffused by grace, so that it can become the medium of God's presence among us. This finds its most potent expression in the Catholic belief that Christ is truly present in the consecrated elements of bread and wine at the Eucharist, but this focus on the Eucharist emerged at a time when a more cosmic sense of sacramentality was disappearing from Christian consciousness in the Middle Ages. Today, with our quest for an integrated and life-affirming theology that can express the beauty and worth of creation, it is perhaps time to retrieve the sense of a sanctified universe that is expressed in the concept of sacramental living.

Sacramentality is a linguistic concept that can take us beyond either an excessive literalism with regard to the expressive capacity of language, or an overemphasis on symbolism that denies the body any role in the making of meaning. Sacramental language recognizes the significance of both symbolism and materiality, situating itself in that mysterious space between words and the world, between language and the body, in order to perpetuate the incarnate presence of God in the matter of creation. Sacramentality requires an act of faith in the power of language to effect material change in the world. Beyond the sterile medieval debates about the nature of transubstantiation, the Catholic belief that Christ is bodily present in the eucharistic elements of bread and wine is an affirmation of this belief that language has a carnal dimension, so that the words we use have physical potency. This does not require pre-scientific belief in magic or mumbo jumbo. It can be understood more in terms of post-modern theories of language, in which language is the filter through which we name and therefore comprehend the world around us, in such a way that matter takes on the meanings we attribute to it and becomes for us what we believe it to be. And if it is possible to believe that inert matter can thereby acquire transformed significance, how much more potent is the relationship between language and the body that produces it, if one sees all theological and devotional language as inherently sacramental in its power to consecrate the physical world?

If feminists are to open the Christian imagination to new ways of speaking about God, this cannot simply be a theoretical exercise. It is first and foremost an act of worship. We need to inhabit the paradoxical space within which God remains the absolute Other, the mystery before which all language falls silent and all knowledge flounders, while also recognizing God as the intimate and self-revealing source of life into whose presence we come in prayer, devotion and faithful living, and also, as I suggested earlier, in the playfulness of theology. It is sacramental language that allows us to express this, because such language belongs not in the realm of metaphysics but in a bodily exchange, wherein we allow ourselves to be drawn into the divine presence, to be known and transformed by that presence, and to know ourselves only to the extent that God reveals us to ourselves.

To say this is not to preclude the ethical and psychological responsibility each of us has to cultivate self-awareness, to be attentive to our habits and patterns of behaviour, and to seek whatever assistance we might need to unravel the tangled distortions and confusions of our psyches and relationships. Rather, it is to suggest that, beyond all the valuable self-knowledge that life and the world can offer us, we are part of the divine mystery, part of God's creative love that sustains us in a constant state of becoming, and what we are ultimately becoming is hidden in God because it is divine. So just as knowledge of God can never transcend the mystery of God, so knowledge of self can never transcend the mystery of my own being. It is this sense of mystery and humility before the wonder of our shared humanity as a way of being in, with and for God, that I believe stands guard over the risk of hubris inherent in every theological enterprise, including that of feminist theology.

In seeking to explore these ideas through the mysticism of Catherine of Siena, I am taking something of a gamble. If the writings of the women mystics are to become resources for the feminist transformation of theology, then they need to be interpreted with critical attentiveness to the ways in which these women internalized the negative images that Christianity has fostered with regard to female embodiment and sexuality. There is a growing body of scholarship that considers the ways in which mystical texts bear the marks of sexual difference. Scholars such as Bynum and Jantzen have drawn attention to the fact that bodily images and associations with food, including the Eucharist, tend to feature more prominently in the writings of medieval women mystics than in those of men, and this was often accompanied by ascetic practices that today would be seen as symptomatic of *anorexia nervosa* or *bulimia*.[9] Jantzen argues that the tendency to treat the writings of women mystics as resources for private spirituality while ignoring the social context in which these were produced betrays the demands of social justice. She writes that in medieval Europe, women's holiness 'was bought at a price which no man would ever be expected to pay: acceptance of the gender stereotypes which made the identification of women with food, the flesh, and suffering service seem natural'.[10] If Catherine's theology offers a language of womanly spirituality and corporeality that is a potential alternative to the texts of masculine theology, it is also an example of the contradictions and struggles that arise when a woman perceives her physical body as a major obstacle in her yearning for God.

From a contemporary perspective, Catherine was a tormented and even self-destructive woman, whose spirituality does not immediately appear to offer wholeness and flourishing in God. Her early death seems at least in part attributable to self-starvation, and she died in near-despair over the state of the Church. But while acknowledging these considerable difficulties with regard to feminist re-readings of her work, such observations also raise questions about the ways in which we allow our contemporary ideas and values to influence our readings of texts arising out of very different cultural and historical contexts, and our willingness to let this be an exercise in mutual questioning and discovery. In other words, as well as challenging some of the negative aspects of Catherine's mysticism, we also need to allow her to challenge us.

Living as we do in a culture that regards all suffering as negative, Christianity invites reflection on suffering as part of life. To say this is not to claim that suffering is ever good in itself, even although masochism has featured strongly in traditional Christian spirituality. We suffer because we live in a world that is not yet healed and brought to fullness in Christ, and Christians are called to be part of the ongoing healing of the world through struggling against avoidable suffering in all its forms, including the self-inflicted suffering of extreme spiritual practices. But ultimately, maturity and wisdom entail the recognition that we cannot avoid suffering altogether, and so much modern science and medicine is driven by a failure of wisdom in this respect. The transgression of ethical boundaries is often justified in the name of preventing suffering, as if freedom from suffering is in itself an absolute value. But even the most protected and sheltered life is vulnerable to the natural suffering of ageing and the anticipation of death, and most of us know that we are profoundly vulnerable to the suffering that arises out of tragedy, evil and violence. No matter how technologically advanced we become in our capacity to control life from conception to death, the eradication of suffering would constitute the eradication of our humanity, for woven into the fabric of our species are complex threads of wisdom, compassion and courage, as well as despair, fury and longing, that constitute the dimension of suffering in the lives of creatures blessed and cursed with imagination, memory and anticipation. So while remaining attentive to the morbid and unhealthy aspects of Christian attitudes to suffering, we must I believe also look for the redemptive and healing dimensions of suffering that are part of the muddled heritage of the Christian spiritual tradition.

Catherine of Siena shares with some of her more modern counterparts – Thérèse of Lisieux and Simone Weil, for example – a sense of spiritual anguish that seems to have overwhelmed her towards the end of her life. Thérèse's last years were marked by a profound crisis of faith, exacerbated by the physical agony of tuberculosis. Weil died because she inflicted on herself rigours of malnourishment and self-neglect, as an extreme form of solidarity with the sufferings of French factory workers during the Second World War. Similarly, Catherine's attitudes towards suffering were much more complex than is immediately apparent on a cursory reading of her work. She committed herself to working with the poorest of the poor in plague-ravaged Siena, and her work brought her into daily contact with the dying. These experiences clearly affected her mystical writings and her attitudes towards the body, and indeed she sometimes seems to revel in images of diseased and suppurating bodies as metaphors for the corruption of the

Church. But while she inflicted a harsh regime of asceticism and self-denial on herself, she was disdainful of such practices in others and urged a pragmatic approach based on absolute faith in the compassion and generosity of God. In other words, she never inflicted on others what she inflicted on herself. But she also saw her own suffering, not as a form of personal chastisement or penance, but as a form of vicarious suffering for others. Secure in the love of God, she believed – as have many Christians – that her own suffering, willingly embraced, could be incorporated into Christ's suffering for the redemption of the world.

So rather than recoiling before the mysterious darkness of some strands of Christian mysticism, we need to weave these into our understanding of what constitutes a mature and integrated spirituality, while also recognizing the many other aspects of the spiritual tradition that offer a joyous and abundant sense of God. Hildegard of Bingen and Teresa of Avila continued preaching and working well into old age and their writings are relatively free of any spirituality of suffering.

In spite of the difficulties she presents for modern readers, I believe that Catherine's writings offer a particularly rich source of theological and spiritual reflection, because they combine a great depth of theological insight with a fluidity of style and a sense of sacramentality that can meet the questions of women today in a space of fertile encounter. So in what follows I offer a brief summary of her life and work, as a way of exploring one potential voice of difference in the Christian tradition, that might indeed be read as a gendered voice telling of a woman's quest for God.

Catherine was born in Siena, Italy, in 1347, the youngest of twenty-five children. Resisting her parents' attempts to arrange a marriage for her, she joined a Dominican lay order at the age of sixteen, and thereafter devoted herself to the service of the poor and the dying.

Her reputation for spiritual wisdom attracted a circle of followers and gained her access to some of the most important people of her time. She is credited with having been influential in persuading Pope Gregory XI to return the papal court from Avignon to Rome, and she defended Pope Urban VI at the time of the Great Schism, when a rival papacy was established in Avignon. She died in 1380, grieving over the parlous state of the Church and in physical torment after months of self-starvation. She was made a doctor of the Church in 1970. Catherine's confessor and close friend, Raymond of Capua, wrote the *Life of Catherine of Siena* after her death, but the *Dialogue* dictated by her and the several hundred letters attributed to her give the best insight into her thought.

As I have already suggested, Catherine's spiritual practices can seem extreme and even bizarre to modern minds, but her theology is the product of what the philosopher Pamela Sue Anderson refers to as 'the rational passion' of women's religious desire.[11] In her understanding of the Trinity, the incarnation, and the relationship of the human being to God, Catherine illuminates Christian doctrine from within by a flamboyant rhetoric of sin and grace, rebellion and obedience, encompassed in a growing realization of the universality of God's love and compassion. Her *Dialogue* is a form of mystical theology that draws on a multiplicity of voices and images of embodiment and desire in critical engagement with the doctrines and institutions of the Church, while being committed to social justice and expressing solidarity with the poor and the marginalized.

Irigaray suggests that, if language is to express the relationship between woman, the body and God, then we need to discover new forms of grammar and rationality. The linear arguments and dualistic logic of masculine reason need to yield to more fluid and multivocal forms of discourse, which might suggest a sense of subjectivity not constructed

around the 'I' of the western autonomous man, but around
the contours of a subjectivity that fluctuates, flows and
shifts to accommodate a more relational and bodily sense
of being. One of the most common and evocative images
used by Irigaray to suggest this difference is that of the
'two lips' of the female body,[12] an image that might allow a
woman to express her sexual identity through speech
patterns not moulded on the singularity of the phallus, but
on the folds and hidden recesses of the female genitalia.
Irigaray suggests that the writings of the women mystics
might be one resource for the construction of this kind of
language, if they are rescued from masculine interpreters
who focus primarily on their incomprehensibility and
quest to express the ineffable, and are read instead as
alternative models of language, meaning and rationality.[13]

To read Catherine's writings with these ideas in mind is
I believe to begin to appreciate the rich relationship
between reason, desire and corporeality that Irigaray refers
to. The *Dialogue* is not constructed as a linear argument
but as a meditation that circles repetitively around key
themes – self-knowledge, love and suffering; the relationship between the soul, the body and God; the eucharistic
body of Christ; the Trinity; the mystical, maternal body of
the Church and the corruption of her priests and servants,
and the universality of God's providence. It is an elaborate
theological construct, dictated and edited by Catherine
towards the end of her life, which brings together themes
and reflections from her prolific correspondence addressed
to a range of people including family, friends, clerics, popes
and spiritual advisers. She presents her considerable theological wisdom in the form of a personalized exchange motivated not by intellectual curiosity but by love and longing
for intimate union with God. The difference between her
style and that of more systematic theology is that it is a
discourse of invitation rather than persuasion, of desire

rather than logic. We are invited to share her God, not because we are intellectually persuaded by her arguments, but because we have become infected with her desire.

Catherine's language is flamboyant and her imagery lush. She evokes the mystical union with the body of Christ in terms of lavish eucharistic imagery of embodiment and blood that are alien and maybe even repellant to some modern readers. In seminars I have sometimes used her famous letter describing how she accompanied a condemned man to the scaffold,[14] in conjunction with the writings of Irigaray. While students have shown a willingness to enter into the spirit of Irigaray's highly stylized and abstract metaphors of embodiment with their images of bodily fluids, they have expressed revulsion over Catherine's viscous evocation of the body and blood of a dying man. This says much about our modern ability to cope with the realities of corporeality, however much we might employ the rhetoric of the body in our academic musings.

There is a paradox running through the *Dialogue*, in so far as its themes of good and evil, obedience and sin, seem at first to be set up in highly dualistic relationships, with the body and sensuality being identified primarily in negative terms. However, these contrasts have to be understood in the context of a more harmonious and reconciling vision, in which the struggle between the body and soul is ultimately resolved in their reunion in a state of bliss or damnation. In the resurrection, the soul receives her glorified body as a gift, and she in turn brings happiness to the body: 'Her own fullness will overflow when on the final day of judgment she puts on once more the garment of her own flesh, which she had left behind.'[15] But for souls that have resisted God's mercy, the body will share in the soul's torment, 'For the body was the soul's partner and instrument in doing good and evil as the will was pleased to choose.'[16]

But if for Catherine the body is an instrument of the

soul that of itself plays no active role in salvation, it is nevertheless the body that allows the soul to express her love for God through love of neighbour. 'Every action, whether good or evil, is done by means of the body.'[17] This means that the body has the capacity to work in harmonious union with the soul:

> when the great chords of the soul's powers are harmonized, the small chords of the body's senses and organs are blended. . . . Every member does the work given it to do, each one perfect in its own way: the eye in seeing, the ear in hearing, the nose in smelling, the taste in tasting, the tongue in speaking, the hands in touching and working, the feet in walking. All are harmonized in one sound to serve their neighbours for the glory and praise of my name, to serve the soul with good, holy, virtuous actions, obediently responding to the soul as its organs.[18]

So often in modern culture, the female body is fragmented, metaphorically and sometimes literally broken and torn apart by its imaginary positioning as a sex object. Our culture represents us as breasts, lips, vaginas, hair, bums, bellies, legs, eyes, highlighting every imperfection. 'Does my bum look big in this?' We are conditioned to go through life seeing ourselves as an assemblage of sexual bits, and magazines like *Cosmopolitan* are deeply complicit in this commodification of the body. For women who seek a more holistic self-image, the therapy industry provides a multitude of techniques, potions and practices that promise togetherness. And if a woman rejects the superficiality of these solutions and turns to the Church for a deeper form of reintegration, she must metaphorically leave her body on the steps outside as she enters. Far from offering wholeness of mind and body, Christianity continues to uphold a moral code and to practise forms of worship that can increase rather than decrease our sense of physical alienation.

Catherine reminds us that virtuous life is a body–mind totality, that our orientation towards God and our active commitment to neighbourly love bring a sense of musical harmony to our souls that suffuses our bodily lives. Beyond her own inability to internalize this vision and make peace with her body, I believe she still offers us a way of imagining and representing ourselves as bodily beings that promises a spirituality of life and wholeness. But this entails recognizing the profoundly social dimension of Christian spirituality. For Catherine, the lonely individual focused on the body beautiful is the antithesis of the beautiful body that is the instrument on which the music of love is played in the world.

Catherine's mystical relationship with God is one of transcendence and ecstasy, but it is first and foremost one that must be actively expressed in neighbourly love. God tells her that 'every sin committed against me is done by means of your neighbours'.[19] She describes God's contempt for those who put their own spiritual consolation before their neighbour's need: 'they offend me more by abandoning charity for their neighbour for a particular exercise or for spiritual quiet than if they had abandoned the exercise for their neighbour.'[20] I would go so far as to say that there are two passions that drive Catherine's spirituality – the first is the longing of her soul for union with God, and the second is her profound sense of social and economic justice expressed in a radical concern for the poor. Time and again she puts into the mouth of God her own furious condemnation of those who, 'bloated with pride as they are, ... never have their fill of gobbling up earthly riches and the pleasures of the world, while they are stingy, greedy, and avaricious toward the poor'.[21] Feminist and liberationist theologies share a concern to expose and challenge injustices in the social order, but this sense that theology must be deeply rooted in justice also pervades the writings of many great Christian women of the past. From the medieval mystics to Wollstonecraft, Nightingale and contemporary feminist theologians, it is as if the social dimension of human life is an indispensable aspect of women's thinking about God. This is perhaps even more interesting if one bears in mind that the stereotypical image of woman is that of the person unsuited to public life and ignorant of the ethical demands of justice, whose sphere of influence must be restricted to the family. Women's spiritual writings suggest otherwise, for they show us that the same sense of care and relationality that inform women's personal relationships extend far into the public sphere as well.

But if Catherine mapped these ideas onto her own body in particularly harsh and rigorous ways, she was, as I have already suggested, pragmatic and generous in her advice to others. There is, Catherine's God insists, nothing wrong in enjoying the material goods of life so long as they are in their proper context: 'After all, everything is good and perfect, created by me, Goodness itself. But I made these things to serve my rational creatures; I did not intend my creatures to make themselves servants and slaves to the world's pleasures.'[22] The material world – including the human body and its needs – is good because it is created by God. It is the human will that gives it ethical significance, depending on whether it is used for the good of humankind in general and particularly for the poor, or appropriated and consumed by the rich with no thought for their neighbours in need. Catherine offers no pious withdrawal from the ongoing challenge of social justice, but nor does she place impossible burdens upon others. It is for each of us to discern our vocation and to live in obedience to God's calling and in service to our neighbour, whatever our status or possessions.

This weaving together of the social, the personal and the physical in Catherine's spirituality is rooted in a sacramental awareness that leads to a complex and multi-layered positioning of the body in her writings. The mortal body is for Catherine a heaviness and a limitation to the soul, but at the same time the body provides an abundance of metaphors for the soul's relationship to God. Her mysticism is not a rejection or suppression of the body, but a symbolic performance of the body that finds its perfection, delight and nourishment in Christ. Thus it is not the mortal and finite body that is capable of knowing God, but the imaginary body in ecstatic union with Christ. This union is described in both maternal and nuptial language. God is the 'mad lover' of the soul, 'drunk [with desire] for her salvation'.[23] The relationship between Christ and the soul is such that 'he makes of her another himself'.[24] At the same time, the soul 'has the Holy Spirit as a mother who nurtures her at the breast of divine charity'.[25]

Catherine does not offer us a set of abstract propositions or philosophical reflections about God. She constructs in words a divinized body that enjoys the most intimate possible union with God in Christ, and through her rhetoric of desire she pulls us towards this body so that it becomes, not simply her own soul in exclusive union with God, but the Christian body that transcends all its mortal particularities and contexts. This is why I think that there can be a fertile conversation between modern women's theology and Catherine's *Dialogue*. Whatever our cultural contexts and questions, we all face the same ultimate questions if we are part of the story of Christ – questions that concern the nature of the relationship between our humanity and the incarnation, what we mean by the resurrection of the body, the mystery of the Trinity in relation to the human spirit, the form of God's love for us and of our response to that love, the ways in which that love

can be expressed and lived out individually and collectively in the Church and society. Our answers to these questions might not be the same as Catherine's, but the questions do not change.

Catherine's soul is a symbolic body, but it would be
wrong to interpret this strictly in terms of postmodern
linguistic theory such as that offered by Derrida, Lacan
and, to a lesser extent, Irigaray, where the body is constructed entirely at the symbolic level with no significance
accorded to the material body in its personal relationships
and social contexts. The difference between Catherine's
highly symbolic discourse of the soul, and postmodern
theories of symbolism, is that hers is ultimately a sacramental rather than a symbolic body. It is physically
incorporated into the body of the Church through the body
and blood of Christ, and it will ultimately share in the
soul's resurrection through its perfection in the risen
Christ. Thus the language she uses, although privileging
spirituality over corporeality, nonetheless consistently
relates its spiritual insights to the body's gestures, relationships and ways of behaving. Whereas postmodern
linguistic theory makes language the site of a performative
and mimetic existence divorced from the ethical and
communal demands of living in the world, sacramentality
seeks to embody the transcendent ideals of the imaginary
body constructed in the language of redemption, within
the material relationships and dependencies of corporeal
existence.[26]

As the quotation at the beginning of this chapter suggests,
the culmination of Catherine's quest is the recognition of
her own divinized self in the Trinitarian mystery of God.
Catherine is empowered, not by way of the rhetorical
affirmation of self, but by receiving the gift of God's power
and wisdom. It is this that allows her to recognize God in
herself and herself in God, as a new creation in Christ. The

fruit of this recognition is the will that enables her to love. These two paragraphs express the inexpressible totality of the Christian faith. They say everything that Christianity wants to say about the relationship between God and the human in Christ, in the words of a woman who experiences the mystery of her own salvation through the discovery of the beauty of her own being.

Yet nowhere does this present itself as a straightforward relationship in terms of the identities and roles of the human and God. Catherine speaks as the daughter, lover, bride and companion of God in an intimate and uninhibited exchange of love, but these are all relational roles that require a constant movement in the *persona* of God as well as in the *persona* of the soul. Thus God becomes father and mother to Catherine the daughter, passionate lover of Catherine the beloved, and confiding friend to Catherine the companion. Such language can take us beyond an ideological fixation with the gender and identity of God and ourselves, to a new sense of freedom in relation to the divine. With this in mind, I want to spend the next two chapters considering the ways in which a woman might situate herself before God in the language of prayer and desire, in order to seek God through the radical abandonment of self in a joyous yearning for the divine.

---

1   Catherine of Siena, *The Dialogue*, trans. and introduction by Suzanne Noffke, O.P., preface by Giuliana Cavallini (Mahwah, NJ: Paulist Press, 1980), p. 365.

2   Jürgen Moltmann, 'The Inviting Unity of the Triune God' in Claude Geffré and Jean Pièrre Jossua (eds.), *Monotheism, Concilium*, 177 (Edinburgh: T & T Clark, 1985), pp. 50–58, esp. p. 55.

3   Elshtain, *Public Man, Private Woman*, p. 105.

4   See Paul Ricoeur, 'Fatherhood: from Phantasm to Symbol' in *The Conflict of Interpretations: Essays in Hermeneutics*, ed. Don Ihde, trans. Robert Sweeney (Evanston, IL: Northwestern University Press, 1974).

5   St Anselm, *The Prayers and Meditations of St Anselm* (Harmondsworth: Penguin Books, 1973), p. 155.

6   Julian of Norwich, *The Revelation of Divine Love*, trans. M. L. del Maestro (Tunbridge Wells: Burns & Oates, 1994), pp. 167–9.

7 Hildegard of Bingen, Scivias III, 9, 25, quoted in Fiona Bowie and Oliver Davies (eds.), *Hildegard of Bingen – An Anthology* (London: SPCK, 1992), p. 81.

8 See Catherine Mowry LaCugna, *God for Us – The Trinity and Christian Life* (San Francisco: HarperSanFrancisco, 1991).

9 See Bynum, *Holy Feast and Holy Fast*; Jantzen, *Power, Gender and Christian Mysticism*; see also Rudolph M. Bell, *Holy Anorexia* (Chicago and London: University of Chicago Press, 1985).

10 Jantzen, Power, *Gender and Christian Mysticism*, p. 223.

11 See Pamela Sue Anderson, *A Feminist Philosophy of Religion* (Oxford: Blackwell Publishers, 1998).

12 Cf. Luce Irigaray, *This Sex Which Is Not One*, trans. Catherine Porter with Carolyn Burke (Ithaca, NY: Cornell University Press, 1985).

13 See Luce Irigaray, 'La Mysterique' in *Speculum of the Other Woman*, pp. 191–202.

14 See Saint *Catherine of Siena as seen in her Letters*, trans., ed. and intro. by Vida D. Scudder (London: J. M. Dent & Co.; New York: E.P. Dutton & Co., 1905), pp. 109–14.

15 Catherine of Siena, *The Dialogue*, p. 84.

16 Ibid., p. 86.

17 Ibid.

18 Ibid., p. 310.

19 Ibid., p. 35.

20 Ibid., p. 131.

21 Ibid., p. 232.

22 Ibid., p. 97.

23 Ibid., p. 325.

24 Ibid., p. 25.

25 Ibid., p. 292.

26 This discussion of Catherine of Siena is developed in Tina Beattie, 'Mysticism and Corporeality' in Regina Ammicht Quinn and Elsa Tamez (eds.), *The Body and Religion*, Concilium 2002/2, pp. 66–75.

9
Woman, Prayer and the Presence of God

Just as I am, without one plea,
But that Thy blood was shed for me,
And that Thou bidst me come to Thee,
O Lamb of God, I come.

Just as I am, though tossed about
With many a conflict, many a doubt,
Fighting and fears within, without,
O Lamb of God, I come.

Just as I am, Thou wilt receive,
Wilt welcome, pardon, cleanse, relieve;
Because Thy promise I believe,
O Lamb of God, I come.

Just as I am, Thy love unknown
Hath broken every barrier down;
Now, to be Thine, yea, Thine alone,
O Lamb of God, I come.

Just as I am, of that free love
The breadth, length, depth and height to prove,
Here for a season, then above,
O Lamb of God, I come, I come!

Charlotte Elliott (1789–1871)

To become a woman in the Christian faith entails being born again, being delivered from a world of closed horizons and social entrapments into the loving freedom of God. It means being able to say of Christ 'in him we live and move and have our being', in a way that does not negate the self but that allows us to discover who we are as beings created by and for love – love of God, love of neighbour, and love of self as the beloved of God. It is to become a new creation in Christ, which is to experience a profound transformation in our symbolic understanding that affects all the spiritual, social and psychological dimensions of our being. To be born again is to change the way we see the world, and in doing this we also change the world itself for we change our way of being in the world.

But the picture is more complex than this, because the Christian life also entails struggle, resistance and failure, not only because of our personal inability to open ourselves fully to the grace of God, but because of the Church's inability to welcome woman as a full and equal participant in the life of grace. I have suggested that in the history of western culture – which is also the history of the Christian faith – the idea of woman has been riven by destructive dualisms. Woman has been the madonna and the whore, Mary and Eve, the feminine ideal and the wanton temptress, the good wife and the prostitute. In between these extremes, real women have led complex and multifaceted lives in the dappled shadows of sin and grace, fear and hope, which constitute the space of human existence.

But as women struggle free of these historical stereotypes to explore and express different ways of being, we find ourselves in a world of ghosts and shadows and dissolving identities. Even as women ask for the first time in significant numbers, 'Who am I? Who are we?', such questions become caught up in the flux of postmodernism's crisis of identity. There is no 'I', and 'we' are nothing more than players and performers in the scripts of history, with our fragile illusions of identity inscribed in the texts we inhabit. If the Enlightenment held out the possibility of universal human subjectivity, of a brotherhood of man wherein Wollstonecraft believed that women too might find their rightful place as rational and equal beings, today we are confronted by conflicting rationalities, fractured identities and the disintegration of universal concepts of justice, truth and goodness. This is the predicament in which feminism finds itself. Woman must struggle against the negations of both historicity and futurity, to become someone whose existence is and always has been open to question.

'There is no such thing as ~~The~~ woman',[1] says Lacan, who puts a cross through the 'The' of '~~The~~ woman' to indicate the non-subjectivity of woman. There is no such thing as 'the woman', for the definite article cannot be used of one who negates subjectivity – shadow, mystery, not man. For Irigaray, the way to begin to assert presence rather than absence, being rather than negation, is for a woman to mimetically assume the *persona* of woman, to discover through parodies and performances of femininity what it might indeed mean to be a woman, while at the same time showing that, if we can perform a role, then we ourselves are not reducible to that role. There is more to be discovered and more to be expressed than the language, values and stereotypes that our culture offers to women, and only through linguistic experiments and performances might we discover the meaning of woman in order to create a true culture of sexual difference for the first time.

Kristeva proposes a different solution to this crisis of identity. She argues that men and women alike need to go beyond the Enlightenment construct of the masculine 'I', to acknowledge that we are not autonomous subjects but divided beings, haunted by feelings of love and abjection, loss and longing, alienation and otherness, and by qualities and characteristics that are commonly labelled masculine and feminine. If we seek to deny this psychological sense of alienation and dividedness, we project it outwards in violent manifestations of hostility and rejection. This, argues Kristeva, constitutes the making of the modern western man of reason – a man whose sense of self is secured by the dichotomy of identity and otherness. The illusion of the rational, autonomous individual is sustained through the suppression of the otherness of the body, but also of the sexual other, the racial other and the cultural other. Thus, suggests Kristeva, the Enlightenment created the conditions for the cultures of domination and repression that have prevailed in modern European history.[2]

Theorists such as Judith Butler argue that gender is a multivalent concept that cannot be firmly secured in terms of the sexual body. The binary opposites of masculinity and femininity are the repressive constructs of a heterosexist society, and the way to break free of these constraints is not to seek a sexual identity as woman or man, but to expose the instability of all sexual identities through the parody and performance of multiple sexualities and genders.[3]

In different ways, each of these three feminist perspectives reflects aspects of the Christian tradition. Irigaray's philosophy of sexual difference is nuanced and subtle in its challenge to traditional concepts of masculinity and femininity, but it involves a complex refiguration rather than a rejection of these concepts, and the sexual symbolism of Catholic Christianity pervades much of her work. It is possible to see her as the distant descendant of Augustine in the context of a tradition that insists upon the fundamental significance of sexual difference to human identity and relationality. Kristeva, on the other hand, offers the possibility of a creative reinterpretation of the Orthodox belief in the non-essential nature of sexual difference, in her quest to incorporate masculinity and femininity, self and otherness, into a new vision of subjectivity in which sexual difference ceases to be a significant factor in human identity. Bearing in mind the difference I outlined earlier with regard to Catholic and Orthodox interpretations of the significance of sexual difference, it is tempting to speculate that these different emphases reflect Irigaray's Belgian Catholic upbringing on the one hand, and Kristeva's Bulgarian Orthodox upbringing on the other.

With regard to Butler, Sarah Coakley has argued that her parodic performances of gender resonate with the language of some early theologians, particularly with regard to the fluidity of gender roles in the writings of Gregory of Nyssa. However, Coakley sees Butler's work as inherently pessimistic, because it lacks an eschatology that would give ultimate purpose to its deconstructive parodies of gender. For Gregory of Nyssa, the mutability of gender allows for the erotic expression of the eschatological body's desire for God. It is this eschatological dimension that Coakley suggests is missing in postmodern theories of   gender, so that they perpetuate the dissatisfaction of western culture: 'the obsessive interest in the "body" which has been such a marked feature of late twentieth-century Western culture hides a profound eschatological longing; only a *theological* vision of a particular sort ... can satisfy it'.[4]

Rather than putting these forward as three contested positions, I want to suggest that a more creative approach for women seeking new forms of spirituality and selfhood might be to recognize the value in all three of these possibilities. There are times when sexual difference is an important and even determinative aspect of who we are, and the life of *eros* depends upon recognizing and celebrating such difference. But there are also times when we do not experience ourselves as clearly differentiated sexual beings, but as indeterminate creatures of yearning and loss, when otherness focuses not on sexuality but on the mystery of our own being in relation to the infinity of the abyss that is God. And we know from the history of Christian spirituality that there are also times when both men and women appropriate to themselves different sexual *personae*, so that the fluidity of concepts of gender becomes a doorway into a liberating world of symbolic possibilities before God.

In this open-ended quest for new forms of meaning, women may be ideally placed in our postmodern culture to speak from elsewhere, from a position of subjectivity and agency that never has been defined by masculine concepts of subjectivity. Historical exclusion can be turned into grace and promise, if we can use this moment of crisis to tell a different story about the person in God and God in the person, expressed not through the personhood of man but through the personhood of woman. This means the creative reclamation of Christian concepts of personhood and sexuality, including a reappraisal of the ways in which the story of Genesis might invite different readings that allow women to draw on the symbolic meanings of the Christian tradition, but from a position in which revelation is not constrained by the need to uphold existing sexual hierarchies.

Recent biblical scholarship has challenged traditional readings of Genesis, by pointing out that the Hebrew word for the first human – *ha-adam* – does not imply maleness. Rather, it is a play on the word for earth – *ha-adam-a* – that is best translated as earthling or earth creature. The sexes only become clearly differentiated after the creation of Eve, when the words for man and woman –*'is* and *'issa* – are first used. Trible points out that the relationship between the man and the woman is described in the same terms as the relationship between the earth creature and the earth. The woman was taken from the man just as the earth creature was taken from the earth. Strictly speaking, she suggests, if this implies a relationship of subordination, the man would be subordinate to the woman just as the earth is subordinate to the earth creature. But the recognition by the man that the woman is 'bone of my bones and flesh of my flesh' rules out any relationship of superiority and inferiority: 'The relationship of this couple is one of mutuality and equality, not one of female superiority and certainly not one of female subordination.'[5] Prior to the coming into existence of sexual difference, when the earth creature is created, it is

> precisely and only the human being, so far sexually undifferentiated. The complete story of creaturehood is a process, the tale that is being told. . . . This sexually undifferentiated earth creature owes its existence to Yahweh God. It is not a 'self-made man,' a patriarchal figure, a superman, or *Übermensch*. Only two ingredients constitute its life, and both are tenuous: dusty earth and divine breath. One comes from below; the other from above. One is visible; the other invisible. Combined by Yahweh, these fragile ingredients unite to form the creature who is totally dependent upon God.[6]

Given the significance of Genesis for the Christian understanding of sexual difference, and bearing in mind the various ways in which this has been interpreted, how might a woman use the readings proposed by Trible to come to a new understanding of herself as a creature before God? Can we read the Genesis story, not as a mythical account of an ancient event, but as a spiritual allegory that helps us to position ourselves before God and one another in a way that constantly invites revelation and renewal? From this perspective, the creative process described in Genesis becomes an ongoing story of creaturely becoming, just as in psychoanalysis, the myth of Oedipus is read as a symbolic narrative that helps to explain the conscious and unconscious processes that continuously interact in the adult psyche.

In prayer, every human being comes before God as *ha-adam*, a helpless being of the dust of the earth endowed with a deep sense of solitude, alone in creation. This is a state of incompleteness, of being brought to perfection and being called to wait upon God to complete what is not yet good. This lack of perfection is not sin but is part of the process of becoming what we are not. Coakley points out that Gregory of Nyssa redefined perfection as 'never arriving' and that, 'For Gregory . . . change does not necessarily signal decay, but can on the contrary mark the endless transformations "from glory to glory".'[7] As primal creatures of the earth, we come into the divine presence and we receive the divine breath as the first stage in the process of perfection, awaiting the endless transformations that bring us into the glory of God. When we accept this graced solitude and dependence as part of God's creative activity to call us into fullness of being, it becomes a sense of expectation and hope that holds us in readiness for what is to come. But to wait in this space of vulnerability requires innocence and trust. It asks us to make the impossible move beyond the alienation and estrangement of the fall, to become newborn and utterly dependent on God to meet us in our need.

Without this original grace, the original solitude of the being before God becomes twisted and starts to assert itself as an aggressive and self-sufficient individualism. The vulnerable dependence of the earth creature is masked by an affirmation of the 'I' as the centre of existence, and this 'I' is male. From the beginning, the Christian story has been played out on the wrong side of the veil of original sin, and the Enlightenment and its aftermath only brought to completion the final alienation and independence of the man from God which began with a one-sided Christian vision of what it means to be a human being made in the image of God.

The rediscovery of the earth creature entails liberating the individual from the illusion of autonomous self-sufficiency, from the ideology of man's priority over woman, and from captivity to the concept of the masculine subject, in order to acknowledge the solitude and yearning, the love and abjection, that Kristeva suggests constitute the truth of the human condition. We experience this as a state of incompletion, of lack that can be interpreted as hope or frustration. Without a vision of what we are becoming, we find ourselves always positioned before our own disappointment and sense of loss. Like the reader of *Cosmopolitan*, our existence becomes defined by an insatiable need to be loved and affirmed by the sexual other, because we fail to recognize that prior to any capacity to recognize and love the other, we must first recognize and love ourselves as the Beloved of God. The way beyond this negation of being paradoxically lies not in greater self-assertion but in greater self-abandonment before the divine mystery. Instead of standing before the world as 'I', we stand before God as a question, for a question always implies expectation and an awareness of the other's capacity to respond. In Christian spirituality, this requires a process of *kenosis*, an emptying of self through prayer and contemplation, in order to be open to God. The idea of *kenosis* originates and can only be understood in terms of the humanity of Christ, whose kenotic self-giving is described in Philippians:

> His state was divine,
> yet he did not cling
> to his equality with God
> but emptied himself
> to assume the condition of a slave,
> and became as men [i.e. humans] are (Phil. 2:6–7).

However, some feminist scholars argue that the idea of *kenosis* is unhealthy for women who have already been conditioned to self-negation, and who indeed may never have acquired a sense of self at all. In what has come to be seen as a landmark article in feminist theology, first published in 1960, Valerie Saiving argues that Christian concepts of sin are modelled around the temptations and failings of masculinity, and that femininity might manifest itself in different forms of sinfulness:

> A woman can give too much of herself, so that nothing remains of her own uniqueness; she can become merely an emptiness, almost a zero, without value to herself, to her fellow men, or, perhaps, even to God. For the temptations of woman as woman are not the same as the temptations of man as man, and the specifically feminine forms of sin – 'feminine' not because they are confined to women or because women are incapable of sinning in other ways but because they are outgrowths of the basic feminine character structure – have a quality which can never be encompassed by such terms as 'pride' and 'will-to-power'. They are better suggested by such items as triviality, distractibility, and diffuseness; lack of an organizing center or focus; dependence on others for one's own self-definition; tolerance at the expense of standards of excellence; inability to respect the boundaries of privacy; sentimentality, gossipy sociability, and mistrust of reason – in short, underdevelopment or negation of the self.[8]

If we understand *kenosis* as a further negation and denial of self, then it would seem that women might need to develop more affirmative and assertive forms of spirituality, while men may need to practise a more radical form of kenotic self-emptying before Christ. In recognizing the

hidden spiritual cost to women of self-denial and subordination, much feminist theology has sought to redress the
balance by affirming the value and integrity of women's
experience as the starting place for theological reflection.
However, although this was perhaps a necessary and
effective strategy in breaking free of dominant Christian
images of women, I think the time has come to bring deeper
questions to bear on the spirituality and ethos of this kind
of feminism in the light of the Christian tradition.

Much feminist theology that was produced in the 1970s
and 1980s was implicitly informed by a post-Enlightenment
concept of subjectivity, in which the autonomous individual
is the defining centre of meaning, and the focal point for
knowledge. When feminist theologians refer to women's
experience as the starting point for theological reflection,
they risk falling into this trap of situating the self as the
ground of meaning, in a way that denies the extent to which
experience is always mediated in language, and a woman's
experience is no more reliable an indicator of authenticity
and truth than a man's experience.

But the idea of the individual as the ground of knowledge also runs counter to the Christian understanding of
personhood. The Christian person is not the autonomous,
self-knowing subject of modern western culture, but a
creature of radical dependence upon God and of interdependent relationships with others. The problem that
women face in reclaiming this idea of personhood is that it
has tended to become increasingly divided along gendered
lines. As Gilligan and others argue, women have come to
be associated with relationality and dependence, while
men have become associated with autonomy and individualism. The idea of *kenosis* when applied to women has, as
Saiving suggests, been used to deprive them of any sense of
self in a way that leads to emotionally and morally impoverished lives of servility accompanied by a constant sense

of personal inadequacy. Women have been taught to come
to God through their husbands and children – through
being good wives and mothers and through a capacity for
long-suffering silence – not through discovering within
themselves the earth creature alone before God.

If women today are to discover *kenosis* as a form of
prayer and of living before God, then we need to learn to
stand before God not as woman or man but in the state of
our primal humanity, as the creature of the earth whose
personhood is still unrealized potential, and who waits in
an attitude of radical abandonment and desire before the
mystery of the divine. The first instinct may be to recoil
from such a proposal, for we fear a tyrannical God who will
violate our sense of self and rob us of our freedom and indi-
viduality. It requires a prolonged struggle – the kind of
struggle for symbolic transformation and rebirth that I
have referred to again and again in this book – to let go of
these distorted ideas of divine power, and to recognize that
the power of God can only be encountered in mutual vulnerability. God yearns for us before we yearn for God. This
is beautifully expressed in the *Catechism of the Catholic
Church*, which uses the encounter between Christ and the
Samaritan woman at the well in John's Gospel as the basis
for its reflection on prayer:

> The wonder of prayer is revealed beside the well where
> we come seeking water: there, Christ comes to meet
> every human being. It is he who first seeks us and asks
> us for a drink. Jesus thirsts; his asking arises from the
> depths of God's desire for us. Whether we realize it or
> not, prayer is the encounter of God's thirst with ours.
> God thirsts that we may thirst for him.[9]

In a thoughtful analysis of the meaning of *kenosis*,
Coakley quotes Daphne Hampson's critique:

That it [*kenosis*] should have featured prominently in Christian thought is perhaps an indication of the fact that men have understood what the male problem, in thinking of terms of hierarchy and domination, has been. It may well be a model which men need to appropriate and which may helpfully be built into the male understanding of God. *But . . . for women, the theme of self-emptying and self-abnegation is far from helpful as a paradigm.*[10]

Coakley argues that feminists such as Hampson misunderstand the potential of the Christian idea of *kenosis* for feminist spirituality. She suggests that *kenosis* can be understood as a 'special form of power-in-vulnerability' that makes it possible to continue 'the tortured battle to bring feminism and Christianity together'.[11] Coakley goes on to argue that

whilst risky, this practice is profoundly transformative, 'empowering' in a mysterious 'Christic' sense; for it is a feature of the special self-effacement of this gentle space-making – this yielding to divine power which is no worldly power – that it marks one's willed engagement in the pattern of cross and resurrection, one's deeper rooting and grafting into the 'body of Christ'.[12]

I have already suggested that the power of God works not against but with women in their desire for a space of becoming that is not controlled and colonized by male power. Coakley reiterates an insight that finds repeated expression in the texts and practices of Christian women's spirituality. The person who allows her longing for God to lead her into a space of the most radical openness and abandonment becomes a new creation in Christ, so that the self that is offered to God is transformed, renewed and given back with a new depth of recognition and understanding as to her own identity in intimate union with God. This is what the feminist theologian Elizabeth Johnson means when she describes God as 'the focus of absolute trust, one to whom you can give yourself without fear of betrayal, the holy mystery'.[13]

In trying to translate these theoretical concepts into the textured language of woman's experience of God, let me return again to the writings of Catherine of Siena. Towards the end of her life, describing her union with God, Catherine writes:

O eternal Trinity! O Godhead! That Godhead, your divine nature, gave the price of your Son's blood its value. You, eternal Trinity, are a deep sea: The more I enter you, the more I discover, and the more I discover, the more I seek you. You are insatiable, you in whose depth the soul is sated yet remains always hungry for you, thirsty for you, eternal Trinity, longing to see you with the light in your light. . . . Truly this light is a sea, for it nourishes the soul in you, peaceful sea, eternal Trinity. Its water is not sluggish; so the soul is not afraid because she knows the truth. It distills, revealing hidden things, so that here, where the most abundant light of your faith abounds, the soul has, as it were, a guarantee of what she believes. This water is a mirror in which you, eternal Trinity, grant me knowledge; for when I look into this mirror, holding it in the hand of love, it shows me myself, as your creation, in you, and you in me through the union you have brought about of the Godhead with our humanity.

This light shows you to me, and in this light I know you, highest and infinite Good: Good above every good, joyous Good, Good beyond measure and understanding! Beauty above all beauty; Wisdom above all wisdom – indeed you are wisdom itself! You who are the angels' food are given to humans with burning love. You, garment who cover all nakedness, pasture the starving within your sweetness, for you are sweet without trace of bitterness.[14]

This multi-layered depiction of the soul in God and God in the soul speaks of the self who is fully discovered only in God, but who in this discovery is herself divinized. Elsewhere she says. 'You, God, became human and we have been made divine!'[15] Catherine is in God and God is in her, and she sees herself reflected in the mystery of the Trinity in whose image she is made. But this mystery is also 'insatiable', drawing her ever more deeply into its depths, not through power but through an ineffable tranquillity and sweetness.

The trinitarian imagery of Catherine's mystical union is a reminder that the God whom the Christian encounters in the intimate depths of mystical prayer is a God of interpersonal relationships, in whose image we are made. The idea of personhood is intrinsic to Christianity, but it is an elusive concept that remains profoundly mysterious. It originates not in the human but in God, in the three persons of the Trinity who live in an eternal exchange of love that flows out into the creative activity of making and sustaining the cosmos. The human creature is caught up in this loving interaction, and becomes a person through the grace that flows among and between persons, human and divine. Thus to be a person – which means to be made in the image of God – is to be distinctive, to have an identity that is constituted by difference and yet that has its being only in relationship. The Father is not the Son or the Spirit, the Son is not the Father or the Spirit, the Spirit is not the Father or the Son, but the being of God exists only in the relationship between and among these three persons, and thus the personhood of God is the personhood of three, and the personhood of the human is also always a person-hood of three – myself, God and the human other. If I am to know who I am, therefore, I must stand always in that space of three – self, God and other – as a question of being.

This means that the earth creature which abandons itself to God in a space of primal solitude, prior to any awareness of personal or gendered identity, receives back the gift of self in intimate relationship with the divine and human other. It is at this point that sexual difference becomes expressive of the loving union between persons that constitutes the relationship between God and the soul. However, in the writings of women mystics, this is not reducible to a straightforward heterosexual encounter between a feminine soul and a masculine deity. Rather, the female body becomes a source of gendered images of nuptial love and maternal care, in which identities merge and flow and separate in a constantly moving play of sym-bolic meanings that do not follow any straightforward logic of gender in terms of either God or the soul. The idea of a quasi-sexual encounter between a masculine active God and a feminine passive soul is a reductive ideology that cannot do justice to the intricate weaving together of images and ideas that informs the writings of women such as Catherine of Siena and Teresa of Avila.

I have already referred to Catherine's erotic and nuptial imagery. God is the 'mad lover' of humankind, an expres-sion she uses repeatedly to emphasize the lavish extrava-gance of God's love. But God also nurtures the soul with a mother's love. Jesus is the 'wet nurse who herself drinks the medicine the baby needs, because she is big and strong and the baby is too weak to stand the bitterness'.[16] The Church is repeatedly referred to as Christ's bride who nurtures her children at her breasts, and I have already referred to Catherine's image of the Holy Spirit as a mother 'who nurses her [the soul] at the breast of divine charity.'[17]

There is a particularly elaborate example of this shifting use of gender symbolism in Teresa's reflection on the *Song of Songs*, when she contemplates the meaning of the phrase, 'Thy breasts are better than wine':

> But when this most wealthy Spouse desires to enrich and comfort the Bride still more, He draws her so close-ly to Him that she is like one who swoons from excess of pleasure and joy and seems to be suspended in those Divine arms and drawn near to that sacred side and to those Divine breasts. Sustained by that Divine milk with which her Spouse continually nourishes her and grow-ing in grace so that she may be enabled to receive His comforts, she can do nothing but rejoice. Awakening from that sleep and heavenly inebriation, she is like one amazed and stupefied; well, I think may her sacred folly wring those words from her: 'The breasts are better than wine.' ... O Christians! O my daughters! For the love of the Lord, let us awake out of this sleep and remember that He does not keep us waiting until the next life before rewarding us for our love of Him. . . . O my Jesus! If one could but describe how great a gain it is to cast ourselves into the arms of this Lord of ours and make an agreement with His Majesty that I should look to my Beloved and He towards me, that He would take care of my affairs and I of His! . . . Again, my God, I speak to Thee, and beg Thee, by the blood of Thy Son, to grant me this favour: 'Let Him kiss me with a kiss of His mouth.' For what am I, Lord, without Thee? And what am I worth if I am not near Thee?[18]

This voluptuous and extravagant imagery might be far removed from the kind of language a modern woman might use in her relationship to God, but it invites questions as to the ways in which women perceive their own sexual, maternal bodies when these are not constrained by the mappings and projections of men. For Teresa, there is no sense of conflict between representing herself at one and the same time as the Bride and child of God, as the infant who feeds at the breasts of a maternal God who is also her Spouse and lover. The female body becomes a resource for the expression of a desire that is experienced as a longing for God as mother and lover, beyond the inhibitions and constraints of human relationships.

I have already referred to Anderson's concept of the 'rational passion' of women's religious desire. In her feminist philosophy of religion, Anderson argues that desire for the divine – particularly women's desire – has been excluded from concepts of rationality in philosophy of religion. She suggests that 'the concept of reason sharply contrasted with desire is too formal or "thin" to deal adequately with beliefs of embodied persons'.[19] She proposes that the 'rational passion'[20] of women's religious yearning might constitute the space of an alternative symbolics, capable of expanding philosophical concepts of religion through the recognition of desire as a valid dimension of rational belief. In this chapter and the last, I have suggested that Catherine of Siena is one source for a feminized theology of a woman's 'rational passion' for God, that leads her to discover the divinization of her own being in intimate union with God. I have also suggested that a fluid and multi-gendered desire for God marks the space of primal encounter between the female person and the divine, prior to any human relationships. But this sense of priority is of course a hypothetical state that we never actually experience. In Pope John Paul II's reading of Genesis, he argues that the creation of the original earthling and the creation of the sexed couple symbolize two dimensions of human existence rather than offering a chronological account of creation. We always experience ourselves as both the original creature in solitude before God, and as the sexed person in relation to the other. So let me end now by moving from this idea of woman as *ha-adam*, as the earthling alone with God in all creation, to the idea of woman as Eve – a sexual, maternal being created to enjoy intimate communion with God, man and all of nature, in the new creation that is the Church redeemed in Christ.

1   Jacques Lacan, 'God and the Jouissance of The Woman' in Juliet Mitchell and Jacqueline Rose (eds.), *Jacques Lacan & The École Freudienne: Feminine Sexuality*, trans. Jacqueline Rose (Basingstoke: Macmillan Press, 1982), p. 144.

2   See Kristeva, *Powers of Horror* and Kristeva, *Strangers to Ourselves*.

3   See Judith Butler, *Gender Trouble: Feminism and the Subversion of Identity* (New York: Routledge, 1990); *Bodies that Matter: On the Discursive Limits of 'Sex'* (New York: Routledge, 1993).

4   Sarah Coakley, 'The Eschatological Body: Gender, Transformation and God' in *Powers and Submissions: Spirituality, Philosophy and Gender* (Oxford, UK and Malden, MA: Blackwell Publishers, 2002), p. 153.

5   Trible, *God and the Rhetoric of Sexuality*, p. 101.

6   Ibid., p. 80.

7   Coakley, 'The Eschatological Body', p. 163.

8   Valerie Saiving, 'The Human Situation: A Feminine View' in Christ and Plaskow (eds.), *Womanspirit Rising*, p. 37.

9   Catechism of the Catholic Church (London: Geoffrey Chapman, 1994), para. 2560, p. 544.

10 Daphne Hampson, *Theology and Feminism* (Oxford: Basil Blackwell, 1990), p.155, quoted in Coakley, 'Kenosis and Subversion: On the Repression of "Vulnerability" in Christian Feminist Writing' in *Powers and Submissions*, p. 3.

11 Coakley, 'Kenosis and Subversion', p. 5.

12 Ibid., p. 35.

13 Elizabeth A. Johnson, *She Who Is: The Mystery of God in Feminist Theological Discourse* (New York: Crossroad, 1992), p. 4.

14 Catherine of Siena, *The Dialogue*, pp. 365–6.

15 Ibid., p. 50.

16 Ibid., p. 52.

17 Ibid., p. 292.

18 Teresa of Avila, *The Complete Works of Saint Teresa of Jesus*, trans. and ed. E. Allison Peers (London: Sheed and Ward, 1946), pp. 384-6.

19 Pamela Sue Anderson, *A Feminist Philosophy of Religion*, p. xiii.

20 Ibid., pp. 171ff.

10
Woman's Becoming and God

For the Times

I must go back to the start and to the source,
Risk and relish, trust my language too,
For there are messages which need strong powers.
I tell their tale but rhythm rings them true.

This is a risky age, a troubled time.
Angry language will not help. I seek
Intensity of music in each rhyme,
Each rhythm. Don't you hear the world's heart break?

You must, then, listen, meditate before
You act. Injustices increase each day
And always they are leading to a war

And it is ours however far away.
Language must leap to love and carry fear
And when most grave yet show us how to play.

Elizabeth Jennings[1]

The idea of positioning herself as the primal *ha-adam* might be a form of symbolic liberation for a woman who has been conditioned to believe that she is secondary and subordinate to man in the order of creation. It affords a space from which to question our sexual identities without being fully defined by them, and allows us to imagine ourselves as solitary creatures of the earth who await the divine breath to bring us to the perfection of our own being. Even in its masculine form, Adam as the first man is a symbol that is less encumbered by negative symbolic meanings than Eve. Although often identified as the source of original sin, there has been comparatively little condemnation of Adam, compared with that which has accumulated around the figure of Eve. It is more usual to refer to Adam from the perspective of the one who is redeemed in Christ, the New Adam, than as one who is condemned because of sin. But while the first and second Adam remain linked together in a redemptive symbolics of grace and hope, the first and second Eve are, as I've suggested earlier, torn apart by destructive dualisms. Mary's virginal purity and obedience are contrasted with Eve's sinful sexuality and disobedience. Many interpretations represent Adam as the innocent victim of Eve's collusion with the serpent, an idea that gains added impetus from paintings which depict the serpent as female, such as Michelangelo's *Temptation and the Fall* in the Sistine Chapel.

I have argued elsewhere that this dualistic imagery is an impoverishment of the early Christian vision of Eve's redemption in Mary.[2] From the beginning, there was the possibility of a mutual symbolics of male and female redemption through the figures of Christ and Mary as the New Adam and the New Eve. I have also suggested that the figure of Eve is too potent to be simply abandoned by women. The task as I see it lies in the symbolic reclamation of Eve as woman redeemed and glorified in Mary, but also as the woman who shares the struggles and griefs of women's lives in the wilderness of history between Eden and Paradise. So continuing with the theme of positioning ourselves before God in the primal condition of our humanity by drawing on the Genesis myth, what does it mean to experience ourselves as woman in the beginning?

Although the first human creature is not gendered, by

the time that Eve is created Trible suggests that there is
an increasing sense of maleness associated with Adam in
the Hebrew text. These are not literal meanings, and we
can allow our imaginations a space of freedom in which to
ask what it might mean in spiritual terms to see Adam and
Eve as the human alone in creation (Adam), and as the
human who finds herself created out of the other so that of
her essence she is a being in relationship (Eve). When I use
the word 'essence' here I use it figuratively rather than
philosophically, not to imply some ontological, predeter-
mined state, but to suggest something intrinsic to a
woman's sense of self, that feels very deeply rooted in
terms of her identity and way of being in the world.

If, as Gilligan and others suggest, men are conditioned
to value autonomy and individualism, while women are
conditioned to value relationships of nurture and care,
then Adam and Eve can symbolize such gendered orienta-
tions. Whether by nature or nurture, whether through the
force of cultural stereotypes or of physiological or psychological differences (or more probably a combination of
these and other factors), men and women in general seem
to occupy different places on the emotional and social spectrum. This is not to say that all men conform to the habits
of independence identified by Gilligan, nor is it to say that
all women are fundamentally relational, and far less is it to
say that all men are masculine and all women are feminine. However, in avoiding such stereotypes, it is important
not to go to the opposite extreme where we are reluctant to
acknowledge any difference between the sexes. John
Gray's book, *Men are From Mars, Women are from Venus*,[3]
reasserts many of the sexual stereotypes that feminists
have been challenging for years, but the widespread popu-
larity of the book suggests that it is saying something
important about sexual difference. I am sure that many of
us have abundant anecdotal evidence to suggest that

women do crave a higher degree of emotional interaction
than men, that women often seem to privilege relationships
over individual goals or ambitions, and that these differences
can be a source of acute frustration to both sexes. Sometimes
these differences are described in the language of vertical
and horizontal ways of relating and functioning. Men tend to
be vertical in their thinking – linear, goal-oriented, single-
minded, directed towards a task or a purpose. Women tend to
be horizontal – making connections, interacting, more concerned with the process than the purpose of their actions.

Nick Hornby, in his novel, *About a Boy*, offers a wry
reflection on the failure of the sexes to communicate with
one another. There is one scene in which Will, an archetypal macho man, finds himself in a pub with Fiona, an
archetypal New Age feminist. Will knows that she wants to
talk about 'existential despair', and he also knows that 'He
wasn't cut out for chats about existential despair. It just
wasn't *him*.' Will 'wanted to find a way in to the conversation that they had to have, but there didn't seem to be one,
and there never would be while he was stuck with his brain
and his vocabulary and his personality'.[4]

In seeking to explore and explain these differences
between men and women, a challenging task lies ahead. For
those who place a high premium on sexual equality at all
costs, there is a risk that the positive potential of such differences will be obliterated in the rush to realize an egalitarian
vision that takes no account of the possibility that both sexes
might thrive better if their particular roles, responsibilities
and desires are incorporated into our social and moral values.
I suggested earlier that Elshtain warns of the need for women
to think about what kind of values we bring with us into the
public political sphere, as for the first time we find ourselves
able to participate in modern society in significant numbers.

On the other hand, I have argued that romantic feminism
shares with conservative Catholicism a strong emphasis on

the social potential of sexual difference, so that women are seen as intrinsically more caring and compassionate than men, and maternal feminine values are looked to as the solution to all our social ills. Yet one need only look at the Catholic Church to see how the highest possible affirmation of women's unique characteristics and qualities can go hand in hand with a traditional sexual hierarchy in which these are used to keep women out of so-called 'masculine' positions of authority and leadership.

But we should pause here and ask if perhaps the desire to have a solution or a goal in mind before we begin the process of addressing a problem, might in itself be a covert form of power that cannot avoid a high degree of manipulation. If I have in mind an ideal that women should conform to – however inspiring or liberating it might seem – I am likely to use a degree of coercion in imposing these ideals as a moral duty. This continues to be a significant problem for feminism. In the 1970s, feminism was a radical political movement, sometimes (although not always) associated with lesbianism as a political choice. Feminist attitudes towards marriage, motherhood and the family were almost unambiguously denigratory – a trend that continues today in the work of some feminist theologians who portray marriage and family life as irredeemably tainted by patriarchal values. Interestingly, while Wollstonecraft was stringent in her critique of marriage, she had a highly romantic and ethical view of motherhood. She saw it as the apotheosis of women's identities, and her belief in the necessity of cultivating virtue in women was primarily concerned with making them better mothers. But modern feminists have been much more negative about mothering, and de Beauvoir was only the first in a long line of twentieth-century feminists who thought liberation from marriage and motherhood were the precondition of women achieving equality with men.

In the 1990s, however, a second generation of feminists
began to reconsider attitudes towards motherhood, as they
themselves became mothers. Also, as feminism has gradually
lost its fashionable appeal, many women are turning to marriage again as a way of life that continues to hold out some
precious and longed for promise. If we think of those readers
of *Cosmopolitan*, the kind of love, companionship and
commitment they crave from heterosexual relationships is
primarily attainable in the context of a good marriage, but
this involves a life devoted to a level of struggle and commitment that is at odds with our modern value system of instant
gratification and the avoidance of suffering at all costs.

David Matzko McCarthy, in his book *Sex and Love in the
Home*, sees an interesting resemblance between ideas of
romantic love put forward in glossy magazines, and those
put forward by the modern Church in its emphasis on the
personal love between husband and wife. Referring to a
magazine titled *Glamour*, McCarthy writes that '*Glamour*
and the theologians share the idea that true love constitutes the true union between a husband and wife – a union
of two who encounter each other face to face as persons.'[5]
But, he argues, 'Good household practices, not romance,
will keep love alive.'[6] He compares the modern notion of
love with the image of love in the Gospels:

> Modern romantics set the meaning of love in the face-
> to-face wonder of wedding vows, but the Gospels use
> the image of the wedding banquet, as a place to deal
> with themes of hospitality and hope for the downtrodden.
> Love is characterized as a turning around for the
> unfortunate, as healing, generosity, and most of all, as
> forgiveness and reconciliation. Grace and forgiveness
> are basic to the theological drama of love. The stage is
> not the discrete context of interpersonal love but
> relationships of the human family and the practical

matters of living well in community. The household, in this setting, is where life, love, and sexual union are ordered to common goods and to God.[7]

McCarthy's vision of the inclusive hospitality of marriage challenges Christians and politicians who seek to defend the *status quo* by appealing to 'traditional family values'. The affluent nuclear family of modern western society, closed in on itself behind walls that often conceal relationships distorted by violence and driven by self-interest, is a very different kind of social institution from that which McCarthy describes. His vision of Christian marriage is of the family as an open space of social exchange and welcome, woven into networks of interdependent community relationships. I admit to some unease with this ideal, because the open house requires considerable domestic labour to ensure a constant supply of food and hospitality, and women usually bear most of the responsibility for sustaining this kind of household. But I also know from my own experience that alternative models are possible. A marriage of real partnership involves flexibility and co-operation, and a shared commitment by both partners to creating the kind of environment in which children, extended family members, guests and strangers can truly be at home. Too often, we confuse this with the need to achieve a high level of material comfort, but it is surely less about one's material resources than about one's generosity and willingness to share what one has.

When our children were young and we had little money for holidays, we spent many summer holidays and Christmas breaks with friends who live in a small house in the country. For us, it was a place of retreat from our lives in the city, and a home from home where we knew we would always be welcome. They too have four children, one of whom has cerebral palsy and is inclined to show her delight or irritation by yelling loudly at the top of her voice. I have many happy memories of the ten of us, plus a boisterous dog, two cats and Lee's wheelchair, crammed into their small lounge for evenings together. We have friends who entertain in more lavish and spacious style but few who have achieved that level of welcome and hospitality. Sometimes I suspect it is because material comforts and the anxiety that goes with providing them can intrude and become a distraction from simply enjoying one another's company.

If one sees marriage as the foundation for creating inclusive communities of commitment and care, then it is surely necessary to see this inclusiveness as a liberating rather than a restrictive social influence. Most of us today, however 'conventional' our own domestic worlds might be, will encompass within those worlds single mothers, gay and lesbian couples, people who are lonely because of divorce or bereavement, and people who are committed to celibacy or have it imposed upon them for reasons beyond their control. Too often, the theology and morality of marriage is used to attack and undermine alternative lifestyles, particularly as far as gays and lesbians are concerned, or with regard to single motherhood, rather than seeing marriage as only one way in which human beings can express their love and commitment for one another and those around them, and the stable married home as a place of community and refuge for those in need.

In fact, historical and cultural studies call into question the extent to which there has ever been a traditional family.[8] Love, sexuality, marriage and parenthood have always been held together more by ideology than reality, with the silencing and covering over of relationships that fall outside these so-called norms, often through brutal and even deadly means. The recent film entitled *The Magdalene Laundries* showed the ways in which the Irish Catholic Church ran a regime of oppression and exploitation against girls deemed sexually wayward. Such practices of denial and repression have too often been used to sustain the illusion of secure family values in western Christian societies.

The theology of marriage is ripe for enquiry and reclamation by women, motivated not by the hostility and negativity that have resulted in the almost wholesale feminist rejection of marriage, but in a more nuanced and careful understanding of both the advantages and disadvantages that marriage has offered women historically and in contemporary culture. In the early Church, the Christian vision of marriage as a relationship based on mutual fidelity, love and respect offered women a considerably higher status than they enjoyed as wives in the ancient world, in so far as it made equal demands of husbands and wives. And if Christianity soon succumbed to a more authoritarian and hierarchical view of marriage that has sanctioned too much injustice and abuse over the centuries, it nonetheless remains true that the Christian ideal of marriage has a very high understanding of the dignity of both partners. From this point of view, I believe that marriage can indeed be a sacrament, in which the sexual love between a man and a woman is nurtured, cultivated and sustained in a way that opens it to the newcomer and the stranger, not only in the form of children but in the form of all who need a space of shelter and welcome in society.

The need for a viable feminist theology of marriage entails recognizing that, even in our fragmented, postmodern, post-Christian culture, most women will still become wives at some stage in their lives. This dimension of our lives requires a spirituality that encompasses sexuality, love and living for and with another, not as a subservient handmaid nor as a feminist *virago* but as a person who has decided to make her life's project a partnership, a shared endeavour of love with all the struggle and inevitable failures that this implies. A healthy marriage is not one that always feels satisfying and right. It is one in which responsibility, commitment, communication and forgiveness provide a sustaining environment for the ongoing creation and transformation of love that constitutes a living marriage. Every marriage, no matter how enduring, is far more about working to sustain love than being in love. In the novel by Louis de Bernières, *Captain Corelli's Mandolin*, Dr Iannis is advising his daughter about marriage, and he says,

> Love itself is what is left over when being in love has burned away, and this is both an art and a fortunate accident. Your mother and I had it, we had roots that grew towards each other underground, and when all the pretty blossom had fallen from our branches we found that we were one tree and not two.[9]

For some people perhaps this kind of loving is a fortunate accident, something that happens in a marriage almost without them intending it or noticing it. But I suspect that for most of us, developing such a marriage is an art rather than an accident, something that we strive towards through years of struggle and tears, commitment and endurance, as well as joy and loving and laughter.

The figure of Eve, liberated from the theology of denigration that men have projected onto her, can symbolize both the promise and the work of marriage and sexual relationships for women. Created for perfect *eros* with Adam, Eve finds herself in a world complicated by sin and distorted desire. If she is to rediscover a sense of wholeness, generosity, love and respect as intrinsic to herself as a sexual being, then forgiveness, reconciliation and grace must be woven into the fabric of everyday life.

But the story of Eve also serves as a caution against

absolutizing marriage in a way that makes women sacrificial victims of an institution that should not be preserved at all costs. Genesis describes Eve's experience of marriage and childbearing in post-lapsarian terms of domination and pain: 'To the woman he said, "I will greatly increase your pains in childbearing; with pain you will give birth to children. Your desire will be for your husband, and he will rule over you"' (Gen. 3:16). If redemption in Christ can and should overturn this culture of suffering and domination, I have already suggested that, in reality, the Church has been one of the most effective agents in perpetuating the domination of women by men as part of the God-given order of creation. But even as St Paul set in place the theology of marriage that would rule Christian theological reflection for two millennia, he also made clear that marriage is not an absolute. A woman's right to practise her faith comes before her duty to preserve her marriage: 'And if a woman has a husband who is not a believer and he is willing to live with her, she must not divorce him. For the unbelieving husband has been sanctified through his wife, and the unbelieving wife has been sanctified through her believing husband. Otherwise your children would be unclean, but as it is, they are holy. But if the unbeliever leaves, let him do so. A believing man or woman is not bound in such circumstances; God has called us to live in peace'(1 Cor. 7:13–15).

Of course, this can simply be rejected as the ultimate patriarchal pecking order, with a father God having first claim over the husband to the woman's sense of duty. But I suggested in the last chapter that faith means coming before God prior to any consciousness of gender in ourselves or in God, in our primal state as the earthling awaiting divine life, and that the life we receive is our own self divinized in Christ. If that is the case, then our duty to God is inseparable from our yearning to discover ourselves as divine beings, created in the image of God and made to be encompassed within the worship of God. In some marriage ceremonies, the couple say to each other, 'With my body I thee worship.' Marriage is a worshipping relationship, and when it becomes instead a violation and an abuse of a woman's sense of personhood, then her duty to God surely means a duty to leave in order to seek out an environment in which she and her children can flourish.

That quote from *Captain Corelli's Mandolin* continues,

sometimes the petals fall away and the roots have not entwined. Imagine giving up your home and your people, only to discover after six months, a year, three years, that the trees have had no roots and have fallen over. Imagine the desolation. Imagine the imprisonment.[10]

Marriage and family life can be the locus wherein a woman's personhood is destroyed, either through physical and emotional violence or through a subtle regime of lovelessness. Domestic violence against women remains a shocking reality in our modern world. That issue of *Cosmopolitan* included a survey suggesting that 40 per cent of the magazine's readers had been physically abused, and three out of four said they knew someone who had been violently attacked by their partner. It also included the statistic that 37 per cent of female homicide victims were killed by their present or former partners.[11] In the United States, domestic violence is the leading cause of injury among women of reproductive age. But citing statistics can mask the terror and pain that real women suffer in these situations. Roddy Doyle's novel, *The Woman who Walked into Doors*, is an often harrowing account of a woman's experience of marital violence:

Being hit by Charlo the first time knocked everything else out of me. It's all I remember now about that time, up to the birth. It became the most important thing. It became the only thing. One day I was Mrs Paula Spencer, a young wife and soon to be a mother, soon moving into a new house, in a new place, making my husband's dinner, timing it so it would be just ready for when he came in from work and had a wash. I was a woman listening to the radio. I was aware that my tummy was pressing into the sink as I was washing the spuds. I could feel the sun on my face, coming through the kitchen window. I had to squint a bit, squeeze my eyes shut; they were watering. I was a young, attractive woman with a loving, attractive husband who was bringing home the bacon with a smile on his handsome face. I was loving and loved, sexy and pregnant.

Then I was on the floor and that was the end of my life. The future stopped rolling in front of me. Everything stopped.[12]

This passage suggests the ways in which violence interrupts the narrative of our lives, destroys our sense of who we are, and throws us against our will into different stories. These are stories that we have not chosen and we might feel powerless to change. They are stories in which we are refused any right to create, imagine or renew our understanding of who we are in the world, leaving us searching for a sense of self, for a sense of loving and being loved and of counting as somebody.

Such violence is utterly incompatible with the idea of marriage as a sacramental way of being in the world, capable of revealing the love between God and humankind, and Christ and the Church. But as I suggested in an earlier chapter, the association between sexuality and violence still haunts the Catholic male imagination in its incapacity fully to recognize and address the problem of sexual abuse. In 1994, Pope John Paul II beatified a woman, Elisabetta Canori Mora, who a century earlier had remained married to an abusive and violent man for the sake of her children. The Pope referred to her beatings as 'conjugal difficulties' and held her up as a model of 'Christian perfection'.[13] Such ideas degrade the woman as person made in the image of God, and they are a violation of women's spirituality when they are offered as examples for others to follow. If women are to create a new theology of marriage, then as with everything else in the Christian theological tradition, there is a task of deconstruction and reconstruction that needs to draw on what is life-giving and affirms the dignity of women in that tradition, while rejecting everything that celebrates avoidable suffering and humiliation as a way to spiritual wholeness. The blessing and suffering of Eve, the reality of her struggle and the hope of her salvation, need to become part of a liberating vision that offers a language of truthful and honest loving in our sexual and domestic relationships.

But if Eve symbolizes sexual woman who yearns for healing and wholeness, she also symbolizes the maternal dimension of women's identities. The Hebrew name that Adam gives her, *Hawwah*, means 'mother of the living': 'Adam named his wife Eve, because she would become the mother of all the living' (Gen. 3:20). When a woman gives birth to a child, she gives birth to herself as a person who must venture into psychological and spiritual spaces that she did not know she had within her. The early twentieth-century campaigner and convert to Catholicism, Alice Meynell, wrote a poem called *Maternity* which articulates the sense of transformation that giving birth involves, even when the child does not survive:

One wept whose only child was dead,
New-born, ten years ago.
'Weep not; he is in bliss,' they said.
She answered, 'Even so,

'Ten years ago was born in pain
A child, not now forlorn.
But oh, ten years ago, in vain
A mother, a mother was born.'

Meynell points to a particularly tragic aspect of maternity,
but even for those of us who are able to mother the children
we bring into being, who are not faced with the trauma of
abortion, infant death or relinquishing the care of our
children to others, we must face an existential revolution
that I believe it is impossible to anticipate or to fully
describe. The biological changes of pregnancy, childbirth
and lactation are in themselves a unique form of intimacy
between two persons, which some feminist philosophers
see as holding the key to a new way of imagining subjectivity as essentially relational and plural. Wendy Wright, in
her book *Sacred Heart*, explores the spiritual aspect of
these physical changes:

One is never the same. After each birth, the body readjusts.
But things are never as they were before. Silver-
webbed stretchmarks are only an outward sign. More
hidden are the now elastic vessels of the vascular
system, the pliancy of muscle walls, the flat pouch of
the once inhabited womb. Each child impresses upon
waxen flesh the unique imprint of its life. Inscribes
one's own life with an image all its own.
    Often I have thought how true that is of the heart
as well. Each child occupies its own space and in growing
presses and pushes out the bounded contours of one's

heart. Each fashions a singular, ample habitation like no other. A habitation crowded with an unrepeatable lifetime sorrow and joy. A habitation inscribed with a name. How could it be otherwise in the heart of God?[14]

Mothering, then, is inscribed on women's lives in a way that has something of an all-encompassing totality about it, and Wright suggests that a woman reflecting on her own experience of motherhood can offer us a new insight into the heart of God.

How often today one hears career women blithely affirm that having a child will change nothing, only to find that a year later they are negotiating anxieties, conflicting demands and divided loyalties on a scale they never imagined possible. We have a long way to go before society offers the kind of support systems that would allow a woman to devote herself to her children and her work in a way that satisfies the demands of both. For now, most of us must juggle our emotions and our commitments in a way that inevitably leaves us feeling inadequate and confused. Allison Pearson's novel, *I Don't Know How She Does It*, is a poignant and witty diary account of a working mother's life, as she struggles to combine a high-powered career in the City with marriage and mothering two small children. The narrator, Kate Reddy, thinking of her children while flying between America and London, writes,

Their need for me is like the need for water or light: it has a devastating simplicity. It doesn't fit any of the theories about what women are supposed to do with their lives . . . Children change your heart: they never wrote that in the books. Sitting here in the front row of Club, nursing a large gin, I feel that absurd organ inside my chest, swollen and heavy as a gourd.[15]

Later she observes that 'Women carry the puzzle of family life in their heads, they just do.'[16] And towards the end
of the book, visiting a friend in a maternity ward, she rem-
inisces about her own experiences of childbirth:

> Place of pain and elation. Flesh and blood. The cries of
> the babies raw and astounded; their mothers' faces
> salty with joy. When you are in here you think that
> you know what's important. And you are right. It's
> not pethidine talking, it's God's own truth. Before
> long, you have to go out into the world again and pre-
> tend you have forgotten, pretend there are better
> things to do. But there are no better things. Every
> mother knows what it felt like when that chamber of
> the heart opened and love flooded in. Everything else
> is just noise and men.[17]

There is a maternal language beginning to emerge in
women's writings – a language of pain and elation, flesh
and blood, a language of the womb and the heart – that has
the power to refigure what it means to be a person, what it
means to be in a world of rights and responsibilities, hopes
and fears, where one's values arise not out of a sense of
autonomy but out of a sense of bodily love and responsibility
for the other. Women are only at the beginning of reflecting
on motherhood from a position of educated self-awareness
and critical distance from traditional family values. This
most profound aspect of women's lives remains largely in
its 'natural' state, unthought and untheorized except in
terms of masculine projections and desires. Although the
cult of the Virgin Mary continues to pervade western art,
music and culture, so that in one sense our history is
awash with images of motherhood, like all other public
representations of women's lives, these have by and large
been produced by men. The eradication of the maternal

cult of Mary and the Church has been a symbolic loss for
women in the public sphere, but we stand on the brink of
new possibilities for bringing motherhood and the qualities
associated with it back into the public domain, this time
through the creativity and inspiration of women rather
than men. That is why I am suspicious of John Paul II calling for women's participation in public life, while remaining so resolutely opposed to allowing women access to positions of visibility and authority in the sacramental and
doctrinal life of the Church.

Sally Cunneen is one of relatively few Catholic feminist
writers who has begun to rethink the maternal Church
from the perspective of women's own experiences and
visions of mothering. She suggests that the Church's concept
of motherhood continues to be one that infantilizes and
disempowers the people who belong to her, and she argues
that, in the Church after Vatican II, we need new images of
Mother Church. She writes, 'Searching for visual images
for this new-old power in the church, I see a pregnant
woman, a midwife, and a housewife.'[18] She continues,
'Pregnant woman, midwife, housewife: these feminine
images and symbols represent the human virtues and
qualities people in the church need to value and develop if
the church is to build a community capable of passing on a
living tradition, responding creatively to a constantly
evolving world.'[19] Finally, she retrieves the early Christian
image of the Church as an old woman:

Old Mother Church rocks back and forth, her eyes
closed. She seems lost in her memories, but she's
starting to talk softly: 'If my children are to learn the
way of love, they do not need to turn to theologians for
answers but rather to become theologians of their
lives. They must give themselves up to that constant
action of sharing that makes us free. It is creation –

perhaps that is why it is so hard for them to let go and mother one another.[20]

In different ways, writers such as Cunneen and Wright show how it is possible to reclaim and reinterpret ancient symbols, to rescue them from their frozen meanings in dead men's texts, and to allow them once again to become suffused with the divine breath that gives life to the dust and clay of human existence. The emergence of these different voices and visions is bringing into being what Kristeva refers to as 'an *herethics*',[21] a maternal ethics that can situate itself in the ambiguous terrain between the law that is the social order, its language, values and symbols, and the fluid, inarticulate presence of the body in all its vulnerability, mortality and dependence. In her essay 'Stabat Mater', Kristeva explores this in two columns that fluctuate between the poetic, corporeal voice of the mother in the left hand column, and the more structured discourse of theology, theory and ethics in the right hand column, as a way of asking how it might be possible to bridge the gap between the two. She argues for a new secularization of maternal imagery, in the context of 'a motherhood that today remains, after the Virgin, without a discourse.'[22] However, I believe that Kristeva underestimates the extent to which the maternal feminine life of the Catholic Church remains a potent source for habitation and renewal by women. For the first time, we are beginning to occupy that space as self-conscious, speaking subjects capable of challenging established meanings from positions that are no longer entirely controlled by those meanings and the men who sustain them. Modern western society has not reached a stage that can accurately be referred to as 'after the Virgin'. The cult of Mary remains a potent source of ideas and images, not only for believers but also for artists, musicians and filmmakers for whom she is a perennial

motif. The question is how this maternal presence can be
reinvigorated so that the values she represents are not
merely aesthetic or devotional niceties on the fringes of
culture, but so that they become pervasive values of care,
compassion and nurture that permeate our societies, institutions and communities with the incarnate presence of God.

From this point of view, the Catholic doctrine of the
incarnation is a much richer resource than most feminists –
even feminist theologians – have acknowledged to date.
Mary occupies a central place in Catholic doctrine and devotion because Catholicism has never relinquished the belief
that to be human means to be born of a woman in a relationship of the greatest possible intimacy and communion.

Feminist philosophers such as Irigaray, Jantzen and
Anderson criticize Christian concepts of God because they
are based on ideas of transcendence and power that deny
the significance of the maternal body in the formation of
life and the construction of identity. However, I have argued
that this criticism primarily arises out of a Protestant
understanding of God that does not acknowledge the
significant difference in Catholic theology with regard to
the maternal role in the incarnation.[23] In her study of motherhood in the Christian tradition, Clarissa Atkinson writes:

> The One of Greek philosophy required no mother and
> was not subject to pain and suffering and humiliation:
> Hellenized intellectuals objected not to the oneness of
> the Christian God but to the humanity of Christ. Their
> conversion, like that of the gnostics, demanded that
> they be persuaded of the reality and necessity of the
> Incarnation, and thus of the birth of Christ to Mary.[24]

The maternal symbolism of Catholic Christianity,
informed by and expressive of women's own experiences of
and reflections on mothering, is ripe for revitalization and

can I believe open up new ethical possibilities that resonate with the insights that inform Catholic social teaching today. For example, the papal encyclical, *Evangelium Vitae*, while maintaining a position on contraception and abortion that many might see as deeply problematic, also offers a visionary and all-encompassing analysis of the ways in which the western 'culture of death' militates against the flourishing of the human family in its sexual, domestic, political and economic relationships. As an alternative, it describes the possibility as a culture of life based on values of care and responsibility for the weak, the poor, the alienated and the vulnerable that resonate with those associated by some feminist thinkers with maternal ethics. As long as women remain excluded from the theological community that produces and authorizes the Church's teachings, documents like *Evangelium Vitae* will continue to lack moral credibility because they are produced by an institution that has hardly begun to implement its own wise insights. Nevertheless, I do not believe that this can or should prevent women from entering into the community of interpretation, from taking seriously the claims and arguments of these documents, subjecting them to the scrutiny and analysis of women's consciences, and making them part of our ongoing quest for new ethical visions.

In trying to go beyond the idea of the primal sexless being before God to think about women in relationship to and with others, I have focused on the roles of wife and mother, because for most women these are still the primary relationships that situate us in the world. Beyond these roles and identities though, we need to discover a spirituality that allows us to express multifaceted identities and subjectivities, some sexual, some maternal, some profoundly relational, others deeply solitary. Whatever kind of relationships form a woman's sense of self – married or single, same sex or heterosexual, maternal or non-maternal –

I suspect that the characteristics normally associated with women do make us more fluid and multivocal than men in our ways of relating.

Men have traditionally been conditioned to see themselves as autonomous beings in the public sphere. The domestic world is their emotional hinterland, and it becomes invisible when they move beyond it. While women continue to be defined primarily in terms of our married status and the number of children we have (closely followed by the kind of clothes we wear and how much we weigh!), men are more likely to be defined in terms of what they do for a living or what they have achieved. For many feminists this is a tendency to be resisted, but I find it a dilemma. It sometimes amuses me when I write for Catholic publications, that they will identify me first in terms of having four children, and only later (if at all) in terms of being a theologian. For many Catholics, motherhood still ranks more highly than academic achievement as far as women are concerned. But if I'm honest, I know that like most mothers, my children are the most important priority in my life. Only now, as they reach adulthood, do I feel that other commitments can come to the fore. The continuation of my studies and then my career have depended on a level of health and stability in the home, notwithstanding the inevitable traumas and crises of childhood and adolescence. I have taught many mature women students who have been unable to continue their studies because of family pressures, and all of them without exception have had to negotiate considerable stresses and conflicting demands to pursue an academic interest outside the home. So these are realities in women's lives, but I am not sure that the answer is to deny their existence or their claims upon us.

Pearson's novel describes the struggle for survival – and almost inevitable failure – of women working in the particularly ruthless and misogynistic environment of high finance. But there is a growing recognition in many places of work that women need their domestic responsibilities to be taken into account if they have children, and that these vast areas of life cannot simply be compartmentalized off in the name of efficiency and professionalism. Life is more muddled and complex than that. I used to tease my husband about the fact that, when he needed to leave work early to collect children from school or stay at home because one of them was ill, he would think of some other excuse to explain his absence – like all the other men in his office. But now there is a much greater willingness to acknowledge openly that, when husbands and wives both work, both need to negotiate childcare and the responsibilities of the home.

These shifts represent a gradual change in the values and priorities of the workplace, although they are still very much the prerogative of professional working couples. At either extreme of the spectrum of women's work, there are those driven by success and ambition at the one end – such as the character of Kate Reddy – and others who must work in an increasingly brutal and soul-destroying world simply to provide the basics for family life. This necessity is compounded by the pressures of consumerism, when children's 'needs' – and the maternal guilt that goes with failing to meet them – extend to designer clothes and expensive technological gadgetry. The sweatshop is not the only place where women are abused by the cult of designer labels. The network of abuse extends from the women and children slaving in factories in the Far East, to the women who walk the streets at night selling their bodies to buy their children the right kind of trainers. Women in the sex trade work overtime in December, so that they can afford Christmas presents for their children (and their 'punters' are often family men with kiddy seats in the back of their cars).

So there is a complex world of injustice and inequality to negotiate in any reflection on women, work and home,

and on the ways in which we derive our identities and our
sense of being – in negative or positive ways – from these
various commitments and relationships. Today we are constantly questioning norms, redefining boundaries and
seeking a sense of self in a culture that has removed all the
markers. For some of us, this is a process of opportunity
and potential transformation. For many, it is a time when
the last small islands of security and love are disappearing
under a rising tide of chaos, and that is also true for many
women who find their traditional worlds of family, faith
and community eroded, challenged and devalued.

But in all this, can there be a coming together, a way of
being integrated that depends not on a clearly defined sense
of self, nor on a cultural melting pot where all identities
blur and merge, but on a new way of understanding what it
means to be human – woman, man, parent, child, sister,
brother, husband, wife, friend – in which difference
becomes harmony rather than division? I can remember
one evening, as a young woman left the van which we use
to drive round the streets of Bristol offering tea, condoms
and company to women sex workers, she paused on the step
and looked at the volunteer who was bidding her farewell.
'I don't know why you do this,' she said, her short skirt
riding up round her thighs. The middle-aged Christian
woman in her sensible trousers and sweater hugged her.
'Because we're all the same,' she said.

This is the kind of sameness that defies the banal reduc-
tiveness of modern culture. It is a sameness that comes not
from reading the same magazines, buying the same make-up
and conforming to the same fashions, but from the deep
kindred spirit that recognizes our fundamental equality in
the eyes of God. No body is more sacred, more precious
than any other. Nobody can buy, package or sell human
life, because it is God's life, infinitely elusive, mysterious
and held safe in that boundless source of love.

To articulate the infinite value and freedom of the human being before God, we need to discover a form of language that is both premodern and postmodern in its resistance to the rationalizing literalisms and illusory identities of modernity. This is a language that invites us to recognize the paradox of the human condition, situated as we are in that impossible meeting place between word and flesh, matter and spirit, the human and the divine. This is the incarnate space of Christ's life, in which every term embraces its opposite and must discover its meaning anew through the reconciling grace of poetry and love. There is an Egyptian text from the early Christian era that seems to echo the sayings of the feminine figure of Wisdom in the Old Testament, and the 'I am' sayings of Jesus in John's Gospel in the New Testament:

> For I am the first and the last.
> I am the honored one and the scorned one.
> I am the whore and the holy one.
> I am the wife and the virgin.
> I am the mother and the daughter.
> I am the members of my mother.
> I am the barren one
> and many are her sons.
> I am she whose wedding is great,
> and I have not taken a husband.
> I am the midwife and she who does not bear.
> I am the solace of my labor pains.
> I am the bride and the bridegroom,
> and it is my husband who begot me.
> I am the mother of my father
> and the sister of my husband,
> and he is my offspring.
> I am the slave of him who prepared me.
> I am the ruler of my offspring.[25]

This feminized reflection on personal identity, refracted through an array of gendered relationships that defies systematization or logic, suggests the possibility of a language that might offer spiritual and ethical liberation from the restrictive categories that have defined and controlled personal and social relationships in modern western culture. Irigaray suggests that this fluid and shifting sense of meaning might constitute the symbolic locus of feminine subjectivity that has been repressed and silenced in the making of the western man of reason:

> 'She' is indefinitely other in herself. This is doubtless why she is said to be whimsical, incomprehensible, agitated, capricious . . . not to mention her language, in which 'she' sets off in all directions leaving 'him' unable to discern the coherence of any meaning. Hers are contradictory words, somewhat mad from the standpoint of reason, inaudible for whoever listens to them with ready-made grids, with a fully elaborated code in hand.[26]

Irigaray presents her ideas as the unique and innovative insights of postmodern feminist psycholinguistics, but her quest for an alternative way of symbolizing feminine subjectivity resonates with many of the writings of the early Church. Ephraem of Syria, whose fourth-century hymns to Mary constitute some of the most sublime poetry of the Marian tradition, suggests the enigma that lies at the heart of Mary's relationship to Christ when he imagines her saying:

> Shall I call you Son? Should I call you Brother? Husband, should I call you? Lord should I call you, Child that gave your Mother a second birth from the waters? For I am your sister, of the house of David, the father of us both. Again, I am your Mother because of

your Conception, and your Bride am I because of your
sanctification, your handmaid and your daughter from
the Blood and Water with which you have purchased
me and baptised me.[27]

As one who finds herself caught up in a myriad of identities and relationships in the incarnation, Mary can
become an invitation to all of us to rediscover the liberating
message at the heart of the Gospel. We are not created to
be trapped and defined in terms of the social and sexual
roles we inhabit, nor can our relationship to Christ be
reduced simply to that between feminine soul and masculine lover, submissive woman and authoritative man.
Rather, we are called to be graced creatures who, as beings
alone before God and as beings who are never truly alone,
are invited to participate in the divine life of Christ in all
its mystery and coming to perfection. As social, sexual and
spiritual bodily beings, we are an enigma to ourselves and
to one another, for what we are becoming is hidden in God.
But we also have a capacity for constant revelation and
transformation, rooted in our ability to give and receive of
ourselves in reciprocal relationships of human and divine
love, tenderness and desire.

There is much in this book that cannot be applied equally
to men and women. History, theology, culture and society
have dictated that we occupy different worlds, separated
by ideological boundaries that have situated the sexes
often in oppositional relationships to one another. But
these boundaries have never been quite as rigid as they
appear. Women have always managed to create spaces in
which to speak and be heard, and men have always been
willing to listen beyond the restraints and confines of the
law. Beyond the divisions of history, what in the end is the
difference between us? Dare we live in the space of that
question of difference, without being driven to formulate

answers that close off curiosity, desire and the continual revealing of otherness, human and divine? Today, we are able to ask in new and unexplored ways what it really means to be male and female, made in the image of God, created by and for love and destined for divinity in Christ. We encounter one another as husbands and wives, mothers and fathers, sisters and brothers, daughters and sons, friends and lovers. Together, we must discover new ways of being together in our fragile and beautiful world.

What can we know, in the end? The future beckons to us from a space of infinite love that we must move towards in darkness and unknowing. Let me finish with a quotation that I found on top of my father's papers the day after he died, copied out in his own handwriting, and whispering of the love that beckons through and beyond the fears and the questions of our finite, fragile lives:

I said to the man
who stood at the gate of the year,
'Give me a light that I may tread safely
into the unknown.'
And he replied,
'Go out into the darkness
and put your hand into the hand of God.
That shall be to you
better than light
and safer than a known way!'
So I went forth
and finding the hand of God,
trod gladly into the night.
And he led me towards the hills
and the breaking of day in the lone East.

Minnie Louise Harkins 1875–1957

Who am I? Who are you? Who are we? Who is God? Hand
in hand with the intimate and infinite mystery of God, we
must go forward into the night of our questions, and await
the breaking of day in the quiet assurance that we are jour-
neying towards our own perfection in the one and the
three who is beyond all, above all, in all and with all.

1 Elizabeth Jennings, 'For the Times'. From *Collected Poems* (Manchester: Carcanet, 1986).
2 See Beattie, *Eve's Pilgrimage; God's Mother, Eve's Advocate.*
3 John Gray, *Men are from Mars, Women are from Venus* (London: HarperCollins, 1993).
4 Nick Hornby, *About a Boy* (London: Indigo, 1998), p. 252.
5 David Matzo McCarthy, *Sex and Love in the Home: A Theology of the Household* (London: SCM Press, 2001), p. 21.
6 Ibid., p. 22.
7 Ibid., p. 25.
8 See Rosemary Radford Ruether, *Christianity and the Making of the Modern Family* (London: SCM Press, 2002).
9 Louis de Bernières, *Captain Corelli's Mandolin* (London: Minerva, 1995), p. 281.
10 Ibid.
11 See *Cosmopolitan*, March 2002, p. 93.
12 Roddy Doyle, *The Woman Who Walked into Doors* (London: Minerva, 1997), p. 168.
13 See Mary Hunt, 'Change or Be Changed: Roman Catholicism and Violence' in *Feminist Theology*, 12, May 1996, p. 46.
14 Wendy Wright, *Sacred Heart: Gateway to God* (London: Darton, Longman & Todd, 2002), p. 119.
15 Allison Pearson, *I Don't Know How She Does It* (London: Chatto & Windus, 2002), pp. 165–6.
16 Ibid., p. 190.
17 Ibid., p. 345.
18 Sally Cunneen, Mother Church: W*hat the Experience of Women Is Teaching Her* (Mahwah, NJ: Paulist Press, 1991), p. 187.
19 Ibid., p. 202.
20 Ibid., p. 209.
21 Kristeva, 'Stabat Mater' in *Tales of Love*, trans. Leon S. Roudiez (New York: Columbia University Press, 1987), p. 263.
22 Ibid., p. 262.
23 See Tina Beattie, 'Redeeming Mary: The Potential of Marian Symbolism for Feminist Philosophy of Religion' in Pamela Sue Anderson and Beverley Clack (eds.), *Feminist Philosophy of Religion: A Reader* (Oxford: Blackwell, forthcoming).

24 Clarissa W. Atkinson, *The Oldest Vocation: Christian Motherhood in the Middle Ages* (Ithaca and London: Cornell University Press, 1991), p. 108.
25 Thunder, Perfect Mind 13.1–14.1 (# 1 of 5), trans. George W. MacRae and Douglas M. Parrott, Nag Hammadi Library in English, rev. edn, ed. James M. Robinson (San Francisco: Harper & Row, 1977), pp. 271–4, quoted in Barbare Bowe, Kathleen Hughes, Sharon Karam and Carolyn Osiek (eds.), *Silent Voices, Sacred Lives: Women's Readings for the Liturgical Year* (Mahwah, NJ: Paulist Press, 1992), p. 263.
26 Irigaray, *This Sex Which Is Not One*, pp. 28–9.
27 Ephraem of Syria, Serm. xi., In Natali Domini, Opp. Syr. Tom. ii. p. 429 in Thomas Livius, *The Blessed Virgin in the Fathers of the First Six Centuries* (London: Burns & Oates; New York, Cincinnati, Chicago: Benziger Brothers, 1893), p. 383 – translation modified.

References and Bibliography

Anderson, Bonnie S. and Judith P. Zinsser, *A History of Their Own: Women in Europe from Prehistory to the Present*, vol. 1. London: Penguin Books, 1988.

Anderson, Pamela Sue, *A Feminist Philosophy of Religion*. Oxford: Blackwell Publishers, 1998.

Anselm, *The Prayers and Meditations of St Anselm*. Harmondsworth: Penguin Books, 1973.

Atkinson, Clarissa W., *The Oldest Vocation: Christian Motherhood in the Middle Ages*. Ithaca and London: Cornell University Press, 1991.

Augustine, *Confessions*, trans. R. S. Pine-Coffin. Harmondsworth: Penguin Books, 1961.
—*The Trinity*, trans. Stephen McKenna, C.S.S.R., The Fathers of the Church, a new translation. Washington DC: The Catholic University of America Press, 1963.
—*Concerning the City of God against the Pagans* [1467], ed. David Knowles, trans. Henry Bettenson. London: Penguin Books, 1981.
—*Sermons 51–94 on the New Testament*, trans. and notes Edmund Hill, O.P., *The Works of Saint Augustine – A Translation for the 21st Century* under the auspices of the Augustinian Heritage Institute, 1991.

Balthasar, Hans Urs von, *Heart of the World*, trans. Erasmo S. Leiva. San Francisco: Ignatius Press, 1980.
—*Theo-Drama: Theological Dramatic Theory*, Vol. 2: *The Dramatis Personae: Man in God*, trans. Graham Harrison. San Francisco: Ignatius Press, 1990.

Barton, *Mukti, Scripture as Empowerment for Liberation and Justice. The Experience of Christian and Muslim Women in Bangladesh*, CCSRG Monograph Series. Bristol: University of Bristol, 1999.

Beattie, Tina, 'Sexuality and the Resurrection of the Body: Reflections in a Hall of Mirrors' in Gavin D'Costa (ed.), *Resurrection Reconsidered*. Oxford: Oneworld Publications, 1996.
—*Eve's Pilgrimage: A Woman's Quest for the City of God.* London and New York: Burns & Oates, 2002.
—*God's Mother, Eve's Advocate: A Marian Narrative of Woman's Salvation.* London and New York: Continuum, 2002.
—'Mysticism and Corporeality' in Regina Ammicht Quinn and Elsa Tamez (eds.), *The Body and Religion*, Concilium 2002/2, 66–75.
—'The Baptism of Eros' in *Theology and Sexuality*, vol. 9, no. 2, March 2003, 167–79.
—'Redeeming Mary: The Potential of Marian Symbolism for Feminist Philosophy of Religion' in Pamela Sue Anderson and Beverley Clack (eds.) *Feminist Philosophy of Religion: A Reader.* Oxford: Blackwell, forthcoming.

Beauvoir, Simone de, *The Prime of Life*, trans. Peter Green. Harmondsworth: Penguin Books, 1965.
—*The Second Sex*, trans. H.M. Parshley. Harmondsworth: Penguin Books, 1972.

Bell, Rudolph M., *Holy Anorexia.* Chicago and London: University of Chicago Press, 1985.

Bernières, Louis de, *Captain Corelli's Mandolin.* London: Minerva, 1995.

Boer, Esther de, *Mary Magdalene: Beyond the Myth*, trans. John Bowden. London: SCM Press, 1997.

Børresen, Kari Elisabeth, 'God's Image, Man's Image? Patristic Interpretations of Gen. 1,27 and 1 Cor. 11,7' in Børresen (ed.) *The Image of God – Gender Models in Judaeo-Christian Tradition*. Minneapolis: Fortress Press, 1995.
—*Subordination and Equivalence: The Nature and Role of Woman in Augustine and Thomas Aquinas*. Kampen: Kok Pharos Publishing House, 1995.

Bowe, Barbara, Kathleen Hughes, Sharon Karam and Carolyn Osiek (eds.), *Silent Voices, Sacred Lives: Women's Readings for the Liturgical Year*. Mahwah, NJ: Paulist Press, 1992.

Bowie, Fiona and Oliver Davies (eds.), *Hildegard of Bingen – An Anthology*. London: SPCK, 1992.

Burrus, Virginia, *'Begotten not Made': Conceiving Manhood in Late Antiquity*. Stanford, CA: Stanford University Press, 2000.

Butler, Judith, *Gender Trouble: Feminism and the Subversion of Identity*. New York: Routledge, 1990.
—*Bodies that Matter: On the Discursive Limits of 'Sex'*. New York: Routledge, 1993.

Bynum, Caroline Walker, *Holy Feast and Holy Fast: The Religious Significance of Food to Medieval Women*. Berkeley, CA and London: University of California Press, 1987.
—*Fragmentation and Redemption: Essays on Gender and the Human Body in Medieval Religion*. New York: Zone Books, 1992.

Cannon, Katie Geneva, 'Moral Wisdom in the Black Women's Literary Tradition' in Judith Plaskow and Carol P. Christ (eds.), *Weaving the Visions: New Patterns in Feminist Spirituality*. San Francisco: HarperSanFrancisco, 1989.

Carroll, Lewis, *Through the Looking Glass* [1929]. London: J.M. Dent & Sons, 1979.

Catechism of the Catholic Church. London: Geoffrey Chapman, 1994.

Catherine of Siena, *Saint Catherine of Siena as seen in her Letters*, trans., ed. and intro. by Vida D. Scudder. London: J.M. Dent & Co.; New York: E.P. Dutton & Co., 1905.
—*Catherine of Siena: The Dialogue*, trans. and intro. by Suzanne Noffke, O.P., preface by Giuliana Cavallini. Mahwah, NJ: Paulist Press, 1980.

Clark, Elizabeth A., *St. Augustine on Marriage and Sexuality.* Washington DC: Catholic University of America Press, 1996.

Clément, Olivier, *The Roots of Christian Mysticism*, trans. Theodore Berkeley, O.C.S.O. London: New City, 1997.

Coakley, Sarah, *Powers and Submissions: Spirituality, Philosophy and Gender.* Oxford, UK and Malden, MA: Blackwell Publishers, 2002.

Cooey, Paula M., *Religious Imagination and the Body: A Feminist Analysis.* New York and Oxford: Oxford University Press, 1994.

Cosmopolitan, UK edition, March 2002.

Countryman, L. W., *Dirt, Greed and Sex.* London: SCM Press, 1989.

Cunneen, Sally, *Mother Church: What the Experience of Women Is Teaching Her.* Mahwah, NJ: Paulist Press, 1991.

Cunningham, Valentine, 'The Hymns were Hers: How Victorian Women gave the Anglican Church its Greatest Hits', in *The Guardian*, 30 March 2002 (http://www.guardian.co.uk/Archive/Article/0,4273,438431 4,00.html; accessed on 9 April 2002).

Daly, Mary, *Beyond God the Father: Towards a Philosophy of Women's Liberation*. London: The Women's Press, 1986.
—*Outercourse: the Be-dazzling Voyage*. San Francisco: HarperSanFrancisco, 1992.
—http://www.mdaly.com/; accessed on 2 February 2003.

Douglas, Mary, *Purity and Danger: An Analysis of the Concepts of Pollution and Taboo* [1966]. London and New York: Routledge, 1996.

Doyle, Roddy, *The Woman Who Walked into Doors*. London: Minerva, 1997.

Duffy, Eamonn, *The Stripping of the Altars: Traditional Religion in England 1400–1580*. New Haven and London: Yale University Press, 1992.

Edward-Jones, Imogen, 'Why I'll always be a *Cosmo* Girl', *Cosmopolitan*, UK edition, March 2002.

Elshtain, Jean Bethke, 'The Power and Powerlessness of Women' in Gisela Bock and Susan James (eds.), *Beyond Equality and Difference: Citizenship, Feminist Politics and Female Subjectivity*. London and New York: Routledge, 1992.
—*Public Man, Private Woman*, 2nd edn. Princeton, NJ: Princeton University Press, 1993.

Fiorenza, Elisabeth Schüssler, *But She Said – Feminist Practices of Biblical Interpretation*. Boston: Beacon Press, 1992.

Fiorenza, Elisabeth Schüssler (ed.), *Searching the Scriptures*, 2 vols. London: SCM Press, 1994 and 1995.

Flannery, Austin, O.P. (gen. ed.), *Vatican Council II, Volume 2, More Postconciliar Documents*. Collegeville: The Liturgical Press, 1982.

Foucault, Michel, *The History of Sexuality*, Vol. 1, trans. Robert Hurley. Harmondsworth: Penguin Books, 1990.

Freud, Sigmund, *An Outline of Psycho-Analysis* [1938, unfinished], trans. James Strachey. London: The Hogarth Press and the Institute of Psycho-Analysis, 1949.

Frymer-Kensky, Tikva, *In the Wake of the Goddesses: Women, Culture and the Biblical Transformation of Pagan Myth*. New York: Fawcett Columbine, 1992.

Gaarder, Jostein, Vita Brevis: *A Letter to St. Augustine*. London: Phoenix, 1998.

Gebara, Ivone, 'Women Doing Theology in Latin America' in Elsa Tamez (ed.), *Through Her Eyes: Women's Theology from Latin America*. Maryknoll, NY: Orbis Books, 1989.

Gilligan, Carol, 'A Different Voice in Moral Decisions' in Diana L. Eck and Devaki Jain (eds.), *Speaking of Faith: Cross-cultural Perspectives on Women, Religion and Social Change*. London: The Women's Press, 1986.
—*In a Different Voice: Psychological Theory and Women's Development*. Cambridge, MA and London: Harvard University Press, 1993.

Gordon, Mary, *Men and Angels*. Harmondsworth: Penguin Books, 1986.

Gray, John, *Men are from Mars, Women are from Venus*. London: HarperCollins, 1993.

Griffin, Susan, *Pornography and Silence*. London: Women's Press, 1981.

Hinga, Teresa M., 'Jesus Christ and the Liberation of Women' in Mercy Amba Oduyoye and Musimbi R. A. Kanyoro (eds.), *The Will to Arise: Women, Tradition, and the Church in Africa*. Maryknoll, NY: Orbis Books, 1992.

Hornby, Nick, *About a Boy*. London: Indigo, 1998.

Hunt, Mary, 'Change or Be Changed: Roman Catholicism and Violence', *Feminist Theology*, 12, May 1996: 43–60.

Irigaray, Luce, *Speculum of the Other Woman*, trans. Gillian C. Gill. Ithaca, NY: Cornell University Press, 1985.
—*This Sex Which Is Not One*, trans. Catherine Porter with Carolyn Burke. Ithaca, NY: Cornell University Press, 1985.
—*Sexes and Genealogies*, trans. Gillian C. Gill. New York: Columbia University Press, 1993
—'Equal or different?' in Margaret Whitford (ed.), *The Irigaray Reader*. Oxford: Basil Blackwell, 1994.

Jantzen, Grace, *Power, Gender and Christian Mysticism*. Cambridge: Cambridge University Press, 1995.
—*Becoming Divine: Towards a Feminist Philosophy of Religion*. Manchester: Manchester University Press, 1998.

John Paul II, *Original Unity of Man and Woman - Catechesis on the Book of Genesis*. Boston: St. Paul Books & Media, 1981.
—*Mulieris Dignitatem: Apostolic letter on the dignity and vocation of women on the occasion of the Marian year*. London: Catholic Truth Society, 1988.
—*Evangelium Vitae*. London: Catholic Truth Society, 1995.
—'A Letter to Women', *The Tablet*, 15 July 1995.

Johnson, Elizabeth A., *She Who Is: The Mystery of God in Feminist Theological Discourse*. New York: Crossroad, 1992.

Julian of Norwich, *The Revelation of Divine Love*, trans. M. L. del Maestro. Tunbridge Wells: Burns & Oates, 1994.

Kelly-Gadol, Joan, 'Did Women Have a Renaissance?' in Renate Bridenthal, Claudia Koonz and Susan Stuard (eds.), *Becoming Visible: Women in European History*, 2nd edn. Boston: Houghton Mifflin, 1987.

King, Ursula (ed.), *Feminist Theology from the Third World: A Reader*. London: SPCK; Maryknoll, NY: Orbis Press, 1994.

Kristeva, Julia, *Powers of Horror – An Essay on Abjection*, trans. Leon S. Roudiez. New York: Columbia University Press, 1982.
—*Tales of Love*, trans. Leon S. Roudiez. New York: Columbia University Press, 1987.
—*Strangers to Ourselves*, trans. Leon S. Roudiez. Hemel Hempstead: Harvester, 1991.

Lacan, Jacques, 'God and the Jouissance of The Woman' in Juliet Mitchell and Jacqueline Rose (eds.), *Jacques Lacan & The École Freudienne: Feminine Sexuality*, trans. Jacqueline Rose. Basingstoke: Macmillan Press, 1982.

LaCugna, Catherine Mowry, *God for Us – The Trinity and Christian Life*. San Francisco: HarperSanFrancisco, 1991.

Laqueur, Thomas, *Making Sex: Body and Gender from the Greeks to Freud*. Cambridge, MA and London: Harvard University Press, 1992.

Lerner, Gerda, *The Creation of Feminist Consciousness: From the Middle Ages to Eighteen-seventy*. New York and Oxford: Oxford University Press, 1994.

Livius, Thomas, *The Blessed Virgin in the Fathers of the First Six Centuries*. London: Burns & Oates; New York, Cincinnati, Chicago: Benziger Brothers, 1893.

Loades, Ann, *Feminist Theology: Voices from the Past*. Cambridge: Polity Press; Malden, MA: Blackwell Publishers, 2001.

Loughlin, Gerard, *Telling God's Story*. Cambridge: Cambridge University Press, 1996.

References and Bibliography   237

Magonet, Jonathan, *A Rabbi's Bible*. London: SCM Press, 1991.

McCarthy, David Matzo, *Sex and Love in the Home: A Theology of the Household*. London: SCM Press, 2001.

McFague, Sally, *The Body of God*. Philadelphia: Augsburg Fortress Publishers, 1993.

Moltmann, Jürgen, 'The Inviting Unity of the Triune God' in Claude Geffré and Jean Pièrre Jossua (eds.), *Monotheism, Concilium*, 177. Edinburgh: T & T Clark, 1985.

Morgan, Susan, 'Rethinking History in Gender History: Historiographical and Methodological Reflections' in Ursula King and Tina Beattie (eds.), *Gender, Religion and Diversity: Cross-Cultural Approaches*. London and New York: Continuum, forthcoming.

Newman, Barbara, *From Virile Woman to WomanChrist: Studies in Medieval Religion and Literature*. Philadelphia: University of Pennsylvania Press, 1995.

Nicholl, Donald, *The Beatitude of Truth: Reflections of a Lifetime*. London: Darton, Longman & Todd, 1997.

Nietzsche, Friedrich, *A Nietzsche Reader*, intro., selection and trans. R. J. Hollingdale. Harmondsworth: Penguin Books, 1977.

Pearson, Allison, *I Don't Know How She Does It*. London: Chatto & Windus, 2002.

Raine, Kathleen, *The Collected Poems of Kathleen Raine*. Washington DC: Counterpoint, 2001.

Ricci, Carla, *Mary Magdalene and Many Others: Women who followed Jesus*, trans. Paul Burns. Tunbridge Wells: Burns & Oates, 1994.

Ricoeur, Paul, 'Fatherhood: from Phantasm to Symbol' in *The Conflict of Interpretations: Essays in Hermeneutics*, ed. Don Ihde, trans. Robert Sweeney. Evanston, IL: Northwestern University Press, 1974.

Roberts, Michèle, *Daughters of the House*. London: Virago Press, 1993.

Rolle, Richard, *The Fire of Love*, trans. Clifton Wolters. Harmondsworth: Penguin Books, 1972.

Ruether, Rosemary Radford, 'Misogynism and Virginal Feminism in the Fathers of the Church' in Ruether (ed.), *Religion and Sexism – Images of Woman in the Jewish and Christian Traditions*. New York: Simon & Schuster, 1974.
—*Sexism and God-Talk – Towards a Feminist Theology*. London: SCM Press, 1992.

Ruskin, John, 'Of Queens Gardens' in *Sesame and Lilies*. London: Thomas Nelson & Sons, 1865.

Saiving, Valerie, 'The Human Situation: A Feminine View' in Carol P. Christ and Judith Plaskow (eds.), *Womanspirit Rising: A Feminist Reader in Religion*. San Francisco: HarperSanFrancisco, 1992.

Shields, Carol, *Unless*. London and New York: Fourth Estate, 2002.

Sobel, Dava, *Galileo's Daughter*. London: Fourth Estate, 2000.

Tertullian, 'On the Apparel of Women', trans. Rev. S. Thelwall, in *The Ante-Nicene Fathers*, Vol. IV. Edinburgh: T & T Clark; Grand Rapids, MI: William B. Eerdmans Publishing Co, 1994 repr.

Thorne, Helen, *Journey to Priesthood: An In-Depth Study of the First Women Priests in the Church of England*, CCSRG Monograph Series. Bristol: University of Bristol, 2000.

Trible, Phyllis, *God and the Rhetoric of Sexuality*. Philadelphia: Fortress Press, 1978.
—'Eve and Adam: Genesis 2–3 Reread' in Carol P. Christ and Judith Plaskow (eds.), *Womanspirit Rising: A Feminist Reader in Religion*. San Francisco: HarperSanFrancisco, 1992.
—*Texts of Terror: Literary-Feminist Readings of Biblical Narratives*. Philadelphia: Fortress Press, 1984.

Viner, Katherine, 'While We Were Shopping ...', *The Guardian*, Wednesday, 5 June 2002 (http://www.guardian.co.uk/Archive/Article/0,4273,4427172,00.html; accessed on 28 June 2002).

Webb, Val, *Florence Nightingale: The Making of a Radical Theologian*. St. Louis, MO: Chalice Press, 2002.

Wiesner, Merry, 'Luther and Women: The Death of Two Marys' in Ann Loades (ed.), *Feminist Theology: A Reader*. London: SPCK, 1990.

Whitford, Margaret (ed.), *The Irigaray Reader*. Oxford: Basil Blackwell, 1994.

Williams, Delores S., 'Black Women's Surrogacy Experience' in Paula M. Cooey, William R. Eakin and Jay B. McDaniel (eds.), *After Patriarchy: Feminist Transformations of the World Religions*. Maryknoll, NY: Orbis Books, 1993.
—*Sisters in the Wilderness.The Challenge of Womanist God-Talk*. Maryknoll, NY: Orbis Press, 1993.

Williams, Rowan, *On Christian Theology*. Oxford: Blackwell Publishers, 2000.

Wollstonecraft, Mary, *A Vindication of the Rights of Woman* [1792]. Harmondsworth: Penguin Books, 1992.

Wollstonecraft, Mary and William Godwin, *A Short Residence in Sweden and Memoirs of the Author of 'The*

Rights of Woman' [1796 and 1798], ed. Richard Holmes. Harmondsworth: Penguin Books, 1987.

Wright, Wendy, *Sacred Heart: Gateway to God.* London: Darton, Longman & Todd, 2002.